THE NAME

הַשֵׁם

DAILY DEVOTIONAL WORSHIP

By Barri Cae Mallin

Cover design and layout by Glover Graphics, LLC @ www.glovergraphics.biz

Vicky,
Shalom!
Barri Cae Seif
Nahum 1:7

ACKNOWLEDGEMENTS

The writing of a book is never done individually. Thank you to Shmuel Wolkenfeld for his patience, wisdom and Hebrew help; Sara Glover who has the pen of a ready writer; my mom Manon, prayer pal Billie, friends Florian and Gail, Dottie and many others. A posthumous thank you goes to Guy Morrell who published Intimate Moments with the Hebrew Names of God in 1999. Most importantly, I thank Yeshua HaMashiach, Jesus my Messiah, my Savior, LORD, the Lover of my soul. Thank You for this privilege. It is not about me, it is about Thee.

PREFACE

"God works in mysterious ways, His wonders to perform"
(William Cowper).

Ten years ago, this book was birthed. Through an accident, two surgeries to repair a broken right foot, I ended up on a bed of affliction for over four months. The previous title was Intimate Moments with the Hebrew Names of God. Today, after contacting the publisher, through an accident, I am nursing a broken left foot. Accident? Nothing is a surprise to God.

There is something about the furnace of affliction. It is not a pleasant place, but our LORD sees us through those times. Trust Him in the dark; He will bring you through to His glorious light.

I shall not try to understand the meaning of the trials, or the reasons for the anvil of affliction. Yet, in the midst of the affliction, LORD, help me to see something beautiful come from the blows of Your hand, knowing that the blows are given in love.

PRONUNCIATION GUIDE TO TRANSLITERATION

a or ah ....short a

ay ....long a

e or eh ....short e

ee ....long e

i ....long i

o ....long o

oo ....oo as in zoo

kh ....guttural sound, like clearing the throat

There is no soft 'g' or 'j' sound in Hebrew. All 'g's' are hard.

ABBA

Ah-bah

"Abba, Father," He said, "everything is possible for You.

Take this cup from Me.

Yet not what I will, but what You will."

Mark 14:36

Abba, Daddy, thank You for giving me Your love.

I trust You totally, even when I do not understand Your Mysterious ways.

Even when it is against my will, Abba,

I thank You.

ABOUNDING IN LOVE AND FAITHULNESS

Rahv Khah-sehd

The LORD is compassionate and gracious,

slow to anger, abounding in love.

Psalm 103:8

LORD, I am so thankful for Your boundless love to me.

I only know love as finite, but Your love is infinite.

You abound in love;

You are plenteous in love,

Rahv Khah-sehd.

Your name defines You: Abounding in Love.

How wonderful is Your name!

ADVOCATE

מַלְאָךְ מֵלִיץ

Mahl-akh May-leetz

My little children, these things write I unto You, that ye sin not.

And if any man sin, we have an advocate with the Father,

Yeshua HaMashiach, Jesus Christ the righteous.

1 John 2:1 KJV

Every day of my life, I want to do right. Yet I don't always

do what I know I should do.

Thank You, Father, for my Advocate,

my Mahl-akh May-leetz, Yeshua, Jesus.

Thank You that He sits at Your right hand, to intercede on my behalf.

Although I don't understand all of this, I accept it by faith,

and I extol You for this most marvelous plan.

Wherever I cause My name to be honored,

I will come to You and bless You. Exodus 20:24b

ADONAI

יְהֹוָה

A-do-ni

Let them know that You, whose name is the LORD—

that You alone are the Most High over all the earth.

Psalm 83:18

This name, Adonai, LORD, is too sacred to even pronounce as it really is.

LORD, Your name is all I need in this life to get by.

I do not need wealth, fame, power.

All I need is You.

You give me the fulfillment

within that satisfies as nothing else ever will.

How beautiful is Your name.

Thank You that Your holy language is sacred.

Your name is sacred.

How I praise You for this knowledge.

May I honor Your life in me, as I journey onward,

desiring to do Your will.

Blessed is the name Adonai.

AFFLICTED

M'oo-neh

Yet we esteemed Him stricken,

smitten by God, and afflicted.

Isaiah 53:4 NKJV

You were Afflicted, M'oo-neh.

Damage was brought upon You.

You lived, suffered, and died to gain us the victory.

How I thank You for this love You had for the Father.

I praise Your name.

ALL

כֹּל

Kole

Here there is no Greek or Jew, circumcised or uncircumcised,

barbarian, Scythian, slave or free, but Messiah is all.

Colossians 3:11

When I have found All, Kole, I have found everything I need.

What a blessing that You are to me.

You are everything to me.

You are ALL I need.

ALMIGHTY

Sha-di

He who dwells in the shelter of the Most High
will rest in the shadow of the Almighty.

Psalm 91:1

How I praise You, El Sha-di, Almighty,

Maker of Heaven and Earth!

There is peace in my soul when I come into

Your secret place.

There is no other place that I would rather be than

under Your shadow.

Thank You for Your ever-present protection.

ALPHA & OMEGA–ALEPH & TAV

אָלֶף וְתָו

Ah-lef v'Tahv

I am the Alpha and the Omega,

the First and the Last,

the Beginning and the End.

Revelation 22:13

From A to Z, Aleph to Tav, Alpha to Omega,

You encompass it all. All combinations of letters cannot even

add up to the majesty that is You.

How wonderful You are;

how marvelous is this plan, Alpha and Omega,

Ah-lef V'tav. How I praise Your glorious name.

Isaac built an altar there and called on the name of the LORD.

Genesis 26:25a

ALTOGETHER LOVELY

כֻּלּוֹ מַחֲמַדִּים

khoo-lo Mah-kah-mah-deem

His mouth is sweetness itself;

His mouth is sweetness itself; he is altogether lovely.

Song of Solomon 5:16

The words of Your mouth are pure. Every word that comes from You

is treasured and divine.

You are pure and always a delight. You are my divine lover;

You are always

Altogether Lovely.

AMEN

Ah-mayn

And unto the angel of the church of the Laodiceans write;

These things saith the Amen, the faithful and true witness,

the beginning of the creation of God.

Rev 3:14 KJV

You are the Beginning and the End.

You are the Amen.

Thank You that whatever my need is—You are the Amen.

I have a need—God is the Amen.

I have a hurt—God is the Amen.

I have an illness—God is the Amen.

I lack—God is the Amen.

I need no other answer—Your Word is the best one yet!

You said it, I believe it. That settles it. Amen.

Like Your name, O God,

Your praise reaches to the ends of the earth;

Your right hand is filled with righteousness. Psalm 48:10

ANCHOR

O'gehn

We have this hope as an anchor for the soul, firm and secure.

It enters the inner sanctuary behind the curtain.

Hebrews 6:19

What an Anchor, O'gehn, You are. An anchor that is

heavenly, that anchors me above, not below.

This Anchor is my Hope, my Teek-vah, that You are

working right now, on my behalf, for the perfect plan for me.

How I praise You for this infinite mystery.

ANCIENT OF DAYS

עַתִּיק יוֹמִין

Ah-teek Yo-meen

"As I looked, thrones were set in place,
and the Ancient of Days took his seat.
His clothing was as white as snow;
the hair of his head was white like wool.
His throne was flaming with fire,
and its wheels were all ablaze."

Daniel 7:9

From before time was, You Are.
Father, to know that You are the Ancient of Days,
Ah-teek Yo-meen, gives me great peace and assurance
for the days ahead.
Thank You for this Shalom, this peace.

ANGEL OF GOD

מַלְאַךְ אֱלֹהִים

Mah-lahk Eh-lo-heem

God heard the boy crying, and the angel of God

called to Hagar from heaven and said to her,

"What is the matter, Hagar? Do not be afraid;

God has heard the boy crying as he lies there."

Genesis 21:17

LORD God, You manifest Yourself to us in miraculous,

divine ways.

May we always know that You even come as an Angel of God.

Thank You for Your Mysterious ways!

ANGEL OF HIS PRESENCE

מַלְאַךְ פָּנָיו

Mal-akh Pah-nahv

In all their distress he too was distressed,
and the angel of his presence saved them.
Isaiah 63:9a

Thank You, Father,
for the Angel of Your Presence who is always there to protect me.
May I never stray from Your ever-watchful eye.
Thank You for all of the dangers from which
You have protected me, many of which
I will never be aware.
How I praise the Mal-akh Pah-nahv!

ANOINTED ONE

Mah-shee-akh

Know and understand this: From the issuing

of the decree to restore and rebuild Jerusalem

until the Anointed One, the ruler, comes, there will

be seven 'sevens' and sixty-two 'sevens.'

Daniel 9:25a

Sheer magnificence!

The prophets foretold of You as the Anointed One.

You are Messiah, and we extol You.

APOSTLE

מַלְאָכוּ

Mah-lah-kho

Therefore, holy brothers, who share in the heavenly
calling, fix Your thoughts on Jesus, the apostle and
high priest whom we confess.

Hebrews 3:1

Thank You for this marvelous plan that when we confess our sins to You,
You are ready to forgive.
Thank You, Apostle of all apostles!
You alone deserve our highest praise.

ARM OF THE LORD

זְרוֹעַ יְהוָה

Z'ro-ah Ah-do-ni

Awake, awake! Clothe Yourself with strength,

O arm of the LORD.

Isaiah 51:9a

By the Arm of the LORD, You performed mighty deeds.

You still do these miraculous deeds today, and will

continue to do them in the future.

How I praise Your name!

ATONING SACRIFICE

Kah-pah-rah

He is the atoning sacrifice for our sins, and not
only for ours but also for the sins of the whole world.

1 John 2:2

Thank You, Yeshua, Jesus,

that You are the Atoning Sacrifice for us all.

What marvelous profound wisdom of God!

Thank You for laying down Your life for us.

What marvelous grace

is extended to me, all because of Your Atoning Sacrifice.

AUTHOR AND PERFECTER OF OUR FAITH

צוּר אֱמוּנָתֵנוּ
הַגֹּמֵר
עָלֵינוּ

Tzur Eh-moo-nah-tay-noo Ha-go-mayr Ah-lay-noo

Let us fix our eyes on Yeshua, Jesus,

the author and perfecter of our faith.

Hebrews 12:2a

When I do not know where to turn, it is a comfort to turn to You.

You are the Author and Perfecter of our faith.

We can walk with assurance, knowing that You have all of the answers.

You author the book of my life.

How wonderful You are!

AUTHOR OF LIFE

שַׂר הַחַיִּים

Sar Ha-Khy-eem

You killed the author of life, but

God raised Him from the dead.

Acts 3:15a

The Author of Life lives!

Victory over death and the grave has He!

We take joy in proclaiming Yeshua Jesus is risen,

He is risen indeed!

AUTHOR OF THEIR SALVATION

שַׂר יְשׁוּעָתָם

Sar Y'shu-ah-tahm

In bringing many sons to glory, it was fitting that God,
for whom and through whom everything exists, should make the
author of their salvation perfect through suffering.

Hebrews 2:10

Hallelujah! Salvation is through You and none other.

You showed us the purpose of suffering.

You never waste suffering.

Thank You that You go before us in all things, preparing us to be
children of God.

AWESOME

Hah-No-rah

For the LORD Your God is God of gods and Lord of lords,

the Great God, mighty and awesome,

who shows no partiality and accepts no bribes.

Deuteronomy 10:17

There is none like You, LORD.

You are Awesome, Ha-No-rah.

In every way, You are Awesome!

How blessed we are to be known by You.

BABY

Yeh-lehd

"This will be a sign to you:

you will find a baby wrapped in cloths and lying in a manger."

Luke 2:12

What an imaginative awesome God You are, to bring forth a Baby,

Yeh-lehd, one who would save us from our sins.

This Baby is the Savior of the world!

Thank You

for Your marvelous plan of salvation for us!

BALM OF GILEAD

צְרִי בְּגִלְעָד

Tso-ree B'geel-ahd

Is there no balm of Gilead? Is there no physician there?

Jeremiah 8:22a

You are our Balm of Gilead, our healer, our Physician.

Your blood is the Balm of Gilead that heals all of our diseases.

You are mighty to save!

BEGINNING AND THE END

רִאשׁוֹן וְאַחֲרוֹן

Ree-shone V'Ah-khah-rone

He said to me:

"It is done. I am the Alpha and the Omega,

the Beginning and the End.

To him who is thirsty I will give to drink without cost

from the spring of the water of life."

Revelation 21:6

It all began with You, and You know the outcome.

You are the Beginning and the End,

Ree-shone V'Ah-khah-rone.

There is great peace in knowing this manifold wisdom.

You were before time, and You will be with me in eternity.

Thank You for this knowledge; it is too high for me.

I rest in You.

BLESSED AND ONLY RULER

הַמְבֹרָךְ הַמּשֵׁל הַיָּחִיד

Hahm-vo-rakh Hah-mo-shayl Hy-yah-kheed

God will bring about in His own time—God,

the blessed and only Ruler.

1 Timothy 6:15a

You are the Blessed and Only Ruler of my life.

It gives me great joy

to proclaim that You are Lord over me!

BRANCH

Nay-tsayr

A shoot will come up from the stump of Jesse;

from his roots, a Branch will bear fruit.

Isaiah 11:1

You are the Branch that has borne fruit.

May I realize that

unless I am attached to You, the Branch,

I will not bear fruit.

I love You, my dear Branch!

BREAD OF GOD

Leh-khem Eh-lo-heem

"For the bread of God is He who comes down from heaven
and gives life to the world."

John 6:33

As there is only one food staple that is necessary for the physical,
You are the only food staple necessary for the spiritual.
How I love You, dear Bread of God!

BREAD OF LIFE

Leh-khem HaKhy-eem

"I am the bread of life."

John 6:48

You are the sustainer of life; You are the Bread of Life,

Leh-khem HaKhy-eem. You are all I need.

Just as the children of Israel fed on manna daily for their life,

I must "feed" on You daily for my life, hidden in God.

Yeshua, I thank You for the example You left us of

daily time with God, for that fellowship is my life.

How I praise Your wonderful name.

Let them praise Your great and awesome name—He is holy. Psalm 99:2

BRIDEGROOM

Khah-tahn

Yeshua Jesus answered, "How can the guests of the bridegroom
mourn while he is still with them? The time will come when
the bridegroom will be taken from them;
then they will fast."

Matthew 9:15

When I think of that day, when I will see my Bridegroom
face to face, there is no greater joy within my heart. I long
for Your presence now, my Bridegroom, my Khah-tahn.
Please give me the patience to wait for You, and the anticipation
will be worth it someday soon. How I love Your name!

Rejoice in the LORD, You who are righteous,
and praise His holy name. Psalm 97:12

BRIGHT AND MORNING STAR

אוֹר נֹגַהּ וְכוֹכַב הַשָּׁחַר

Or No-gah V'Kho-khav Hah-Shah-khahr

"I, Yeshua, Jesus, have sent My angel to give you this
testimony for the churches. I am the Root and the
Offspring of David, and the bright Morning Star."

Revelation 22:16

Father, how I thank You so much for the Bright and
Morning Star, Or No-gah V'kho-khav Hah-Shah-khahr.
I call Him Yeshua, I call Him Jesus, my Savior and LORD.
I thank You that He goes before me in all I do, to bring
light to my path, to show me the way, to help me carry
my burden. Thank You for Him; He is All to me.

BRIGHTNESS OF HIS GLORY

זֹהַר כְּבוֹדוֹ

Zo-har K'vo-do

Who being the brightness of His glory, and the express
image of His person, and upholding all things by the word
of His power, when He had by Himself purged our sins,
sat down on the right hand of the Majesty on high.

Hebrews 1:3 KJV

What a wonder You are! Indescribable light, and Light from
Light. You are the express image of God, yet You humbled
Yourself to become as man, that we could become rich in God.
Thank You, God, for this wonderful plan about Yeshua
Jesus, whom You loved so much that any and all who believe
in Him will never perish, but will have eternal life. How I praise
You, the Brightness of His Glory, Zo-har K'vo-do.

Yet He saved them for His name's sake, to make
His mighty power known. Psalm 106:8

BRONZE SNAKE

נְחַשׁ נְחֹשֶׁת

N'khahsh N'khoh-sheht

So Moses made a bronze snake and put it up on a pole.

Then when anyone was bitten by a snake

and looked at the bronze snake, he lived.

Numbers 21:9

Our finite minds will never understand this principle:

that which was deadly, gave life.

The cross, the tree upon which You died, although deadly, brings life.

Thank You that You are that Bronze Snake, the N'khahsh N'khah-sheht.

Thank You for the healing I receive when I look at You.

CAPSTONE

רֹאשׁ פִּנָּה

Rosh Pee-nah

The stone the builders rejected has become the capstone.

Psalm 118:22

You are the Capstone, the only foundation that truly

matters in life. May I always seek to build my life

upon You, Your word, Your truth.

CAPTAIN OF THE HOST OF THE LORD

שַׂר-צְבָא-יְהוָה

Sahr Ts'vah Ah-don-i

And it came to pass, when Joshua was by Jericho, that
he lifted up his eyes and looked, and behold, there stood a
man over against him with his sword drawn in his hand:
and Joshua went unto him, and said unto him,
Art thou for us, or for our adversaries?
And he said, Nay; but as captain of the host of the LORD
am I now come.

Joshua 5:13-14a KJV

O LORD, how many are my adversaries! Yet You are always
around me, to offer protection. You are Sahr Ts'vah Ah-don-i,
Captain of the Host of the LORD.
Thank You that even though
You are sometimes concealed, You are ever-present.
How I love Your name.

CARPENTER'S SON

Ben Heh-Khah-rahsh

"Isn't this the carpenter's son? Isn't His mother's
name Mary, and aren't His brothers
James, Joseph, Simon and Judas?"
Matthew 13:55

I pray that I will never have shallow thinking about
You, LORD. May I never put You in a box.
You are the LORD of heaven,
so much more than a Carpenter's Son,
Ben Heh-Khah-rahsh.
May I never limit You;
may I never limit Your work in my life.
Thank You for Your boundless love.

And whatever You do, whether in word or deed, do it all
in the name of the Lord Jesus, giving thanks
to God the Father through Him.
Colossians 3:17

CHIEF SHEPHERD

אַבִּיר הָרֹעִים

Ah-beer Hah-ro-eem

And when the Chief Shepherd appears,
You will receive the crown of glory
that will never fade away.

1 Peter 5:4

What a comfort it is to know that You are my
Chief Shepherd! I confess my sheepishness to
You and proclaim my desire is to follow only You!

CHOSEN OF GOD

בְּחִיר הָאֱלֹהִים

B'kheer Ha Eh-lo-heem

And the people stood beholding. And rulers also
with them derided Him, saying, He saved others;
let Him save Himself, if He be Christ Mashiach, the
chosen of God. Luke 23:35 KJV

You truly are Chosen of God, B'kheer Ha Eh-lo-heem.
No one could have endured that which You did,
all because of love. How I praise You, Yeshua Jesus,
for You endured all pain, all sins—all because of love.
How I praise God for His Chosen.

Then the LORD came down in the cloud and stood there with
him and proclaimed His name, the LORD.
Exodus 34:5

CONFIDENCE OF ALL THE ENDS OF THE EARTH

מִבְטָח כָּל-קַצְוֵי-אֶרֶץ

Meev-takh Kole Kahtz-vay Eh-retz

By awesome deeds in righteousness You will answer us,

O God of our salvation,

You who are the confidence of all the ends of the earth.

Psalm 65:5a NKJV

When I don't have confidence in myself, all I have to do is look up to You.

You are the Confidence of All the Ends of the Earth,

Meev-takh Kole Kahtz-vay Eh-retz.

What a comfort and assurance it is to know that

You have everything under control.

How I praise Your glorious name!

At that time men began to call on the name of the LORD.

Genesis 4:26b

CONSOLATION OF ISRAEL

נֶחָמַת יִשְׂרָאֵל

Neh-khah-maht Yees-rah-el

Now there was a man in Jerusalem called Simeon,

who was righteous and devout. He was waiting for

the consolation of Israel,

and the Holy Spirit was upon him.

Luke 2:25

Simeon recognized You, even as a little Baby, as the

Consolation of Israel, Neh-khah-maht Yees-rah-el.

You are our Helper, Guide, and Lover of our soul.

You are everything,

and You bring the most comfort in the midst of the storm.

How I love Your name.

They must be holy to their God and must not profane the
name of their God. Leviticus 21:6a

CONSUMING FIRE

אֵשׁ אֹכְלָה

Aysh Okh-lah

"For our God is a consuming fire."

Hebrews 12:29

How I praise You, for You do not desire just part of me:

You desire all of me.

You want the whole, not the part.

You are a Consuming Fire, Aysh Okh-lah.

And when You place Your touch of fire upon me,

You purify all areas of My life,

getting rid of the dross to bring forth gold.

In the furnace of affliction,

You are all I need, O Consuming Fire.

COUNSELOR

Yo-ayts

For to us a child is born,

to us a son is given,

and the government will be on His shoulders.

And He will be called

Wonderful Counselor.

Isaiah 9:6a

Dear Father,

Your counsel rules over all earthly machinations.

You are Sovereign.

I am thankful that I can come to You for the best counsel.

Thank You for this wisdom from above—from You.

Help me to have ears to hear, and a heart ready to accept.

I thank You for being the best Counselor, Yo-ayts.

CREATOR

בּוֹרֵא

Bo-ray

Do You not know? Have you not heard?

The LORD is the everlasting God,

the Creator of the ends of the earth.

He will not grow tired or weary,

and His understanding no one can fathom.

Isaiah 40:28

What a blessing to know that You, the Creator of all, know me!

There is nothing more profound than to know that You know me,

You created me, and You love me!

CREATOR OF HEAVEN AND EARTH

קֹנֵה שָׁמַיִם וָאָרֶץ

Ko-nay Shah-mi-yeem Vah-ah-rehts

Then Melchizedek, king of Salem, brought out bread and wine.

he was priest of God Most High, and he blessed Abram, saying,

"Blessed be Abram by God Most High,

Creator of heaven and earth."

Genesis 14:18-19

You, Creator of Heaven and Earth, care for me.

You, who were there before time began—You love me.

Thank You for this gift of Your love; it is timeless and eternal.

I will always be with You, here on earth and in heaven.

I can think of no greater gift,

Ko-nay Shah-mi-yeem Vah-ah-rets,

Creator of Heaven and Earth.

So He became as much superior to the angels as the name
He has inherited is superior to theirs. Hebrews 1:4

CREATOR OF THE ENDS OF THE EARTH

בּוֹרֵא קְצוֹת הָאָרֶץ

Bo-ray K'tsot Ha-ah-rets

Do you not know? Have you not heard? The
LORD is the everlasting God, the Creator of the
ends of the earth. He will not grow tired or weary,
and His understanding no one can fathom.

Isaiah 40:28

Where are the ends of the earth? Even if I find myself
there, I need not be concerned—because You are there,
Creator of the Ends of the Earth, Bo-ray K'tsot Ha-ah-rets.
What a comfort to know that wherever I am, You are with me.
How I love Your name!

CRUSHED

M'doo-khah

But He was pierced for our transgressions,

He was crushed for our iniquities.

Isaiah 53:5a

How did You endure?

You were Crushed, M'doo-khah, for me, for my sin.

You took the penalty that I deserved.

I owe You my life.

Thank You for allowing me to live this exchanged life.

You took my place so that I may live.

CUT OFF

נִגְזַר

Neeg-tsahr

For He was cut off from the land of the living;

for the transgressions of my people He was stricken.

Isaiah 53:8b

You were Cut Off from living, Neeg-tsahr.

You were sentenced, yet You did nothing wrong.

What an example You are to me.

Thank You for Your love for me.

DAYSPRING

אוֹרבֹּֽקֶר

Or Bo-kehr

Through the tender mercy of our God;

whereby the dayspring from on high

hath visited us.

Luke 1:78 KJV

You are the light of the morning, the Dayspring,

Or Bo-kehr. Your presence sheds light on all

darkness, and Your mercy covers all.

How thankful I am to know You,

to know Your mercy and

Your lovingkindness.

I need nothing else other than You.

How wonderful is Your name.

Then all the peoples on earth shall see that You are

called by the name of the LORD, and they will fear You.

Deuteronomy 28:10

DEFENDER OF WIDOWS

דִּין אַלְמָנוֹת

Dah-yahn Ahl-mah-note

A father to the fatherless,

Psalm 68:5

What a blessing it is to be defended by You.
There is no better defense, Defender of Widows,
Dah-yahn Ahl-mah-note.

DELIVERER

Go-ale

And so all Israel will be saved, as it is written:

"The deliverer will come from Zion;

He will turn godlessness away from Jacob."

Romans 11:26

I praise You, my Deliverer, for always coming to my rescue.

I have no need to fear, for You are always

standing by to help. How I praise Your name!

DESIRE OF OUR SOUL

תַּאֲוַת-נָפֶשׁ

Tah-ah-vaht Nah-fehsh

Yea, in the way of Thy judgments, O LORD,

have we waited for Thee;

the desire of our soul is to Thy name,

and to the remembrance of Thee.

Isaiah 26:8 KJV

You are the Desire of my Soul, Tah-ah-vaht Nah-fehsh.

You are the only one whom I desire; You know me

inside and out, and You know what makes me tick.

Who else do I have on earth but Thee,

and who else do I need on earth but Thee?

I need no one but You.

How I love Your name!

DESIRED OF ALL NATIONS

חֶמְדַּת כָּל-הַגּוֹיִם

Khehm-daht kol Hah-goy-eem

"I will shake all nations, and the desired of all nations will come, and I will fill this house with glory," says the LORD Almighty.

Haggai 2:7

You, the Desired of All Nations, will one day come for Your Beloved. May we be ready and prepared.

"Do not swear falsely by My name
and so profane the name of
Your God. I am the Lord."

Leviticus 19:12

DESPISED

Neev-zeh

He was despised and rejected by men,
a man of sorrows, and familiar with suffering.

Isaiah 53:3a

As much as I hate to admit it,

You were Despised, Neev-zeh, by men.

Would I have been there in that crowd?

The thought makes me shudder. But today,

yes, today, I love You, and You are desired.

DIVINE LONGSUFFERING

אֱלֹהִים בְּאֹרֶךְ אַפּוֹ

Eh-lo-heem B'o-rehkh Ah-poe

. . .who formerly were disobedient, when once the Divine longsuffering

waited in the days of Noah, while the ark was being prepared, in which a few,

that is, eight souls, were saved through water.

1 Peter 3:20 NKJV

When I want to be angry in my waiting,

may I always focus on You,

who are the Divine Longsuffering.

Thank You for

Your infinite divine patience with me.

"Because he loves Me," says the LORD, "I will rescue him;

I will protect him, for he acknowledges My name." Psalm 91:14

ETERNAL GOD

Eh-lo-hay Keh-dehm

The eternal God is Your refuge,

and underneath are the everlasting arms.

Deuteronomy 33:27a

From eternity to eternity, You are God.

I want no other refuge but You, my Eternal God.

What a peace it is to know that

You know times past and You know times future.

I put my hope in You, Eternal God.

ETERNAL LIFE

חַיֵּי־עַד

Khy-yay Ahd

We know also that the Son of God has come and has given us understanding,

so that we may know Him who is true.

And we are in Him who is true—even in His Son Jesus Christ,

Yeshua HaMashiach.

He is the true God and eternal life.

1 John 5:20

The human mind cannot comprehend the vastness of Eternal Life.

Thank You that You are in tomorrow and

You are in eternity.

This brings me great peace. I praise Your name.

EVER-PRESENT HELP IN TROUBLE

עֶזְרָה בְצָרוֹת
נִמְצָא מְאֹד

Ez-rah V'tsah-rot Neem-tsah M'od

God is our refuge and strength,

an ever-present help in trouble.

Psalm 46:1

Father, how I praise Your name

for always being a shield about me.

You are my Ever-Present Help in Trouble

and also in peace.

Thank You that You are always there

to come to my defense. When foes rise up against me,

You always help me. May I always remember this name of Yours,

Ez-rah V'tsah-rot Neem-tsah M'od,

Ever-Present Help in Trouble.

EVERLASTING FATHER

אֲבִי-עַד

Ah-vee Ahd

For to us a child is born, to us a son is given,

and the government will be on His shoulders.

And He will be called Wonderful Counselor,

Mighty God, Everlasting Father, Prince of Peace.

Isaiah 9:6

How it comforts my soul to know that

You are my Everlasting Father.

Though my earthly father has limited time on earth,

You are there for me forever.

How I praise Your name!

EVERLASTING GOD

אֵל עוֹלָם

El O-lahm

Then Abraham planted a tamarisk tree in Beersheba,

and there called on the name of the LORD,

the Everlasting God.

Genesis 21:33 NKJV

You were there at my birth;

You will be there at my death.

Thank You, LORD, that You even recorded

Abraham's tree planting.

Thank You that even the smallest thing done in Your name

will not go unnoticed by You.

How I praise You, my Everlasting God, El O-lahm.

From the rising of the sun to the place where it sets,

the name of the LORD is to be praised. Psalm 113:3

FAITHFUL AND TRUE WITNESS

עֵד הָאֱמֶת
וְהַצֶּדֶק

Aid Hah-Eh-meht V'hah-tseh-dehk

"To the angel of the church in Laodicea write:

These are the words of the Amen,

the faithful and true witness,

the ruler of God's creation."

Revelation 3:14

To be faithful and true is a rare combination these days,

yet You are all that plus more.

Whenever I am in trouble,

I am so glad that it is You, the Faithful and True Witness,

Aid Hah-Eh-meht V'hah-tseh-dehk, who comes to my rescue.

I need no one else but You. Thank You, LORD!

"Praise be to the name of God for ever and ever." Daniel 2:20a

FAMILIAR WITH SUFFERING

וִידוּעַ חֹלִי

Vee-du-ah Kho-lee

He was despised and rejected by men,

a man of sorrows, and familiar with suffering.

Isaiah 53:3a

My dear Yeshua,

all I can say is,

Thank You for dying for me.

Thank You that I have One whom I can follow who is

Familiar with Suffering, Vee-du-ah Kho-lee.

What a help it is to know You are with me in those sad times.

FATHER

Ah-vee

He will call out to me,

"You are my Father, my God, the Rock my Savior."

Psalm 89:26

There is nothing more comforting to me than to know that

You are my Father, Ah-vee.

Thank You for the miraculous ways that You provide for me!

Thank You for the many ways that You shower me with

Father love.

Please forgive me for my childish outbursts, for deep down,

I know that You, Father, Ah-vee, know best.

Let them praise His name with dancing

and make music to Him with tambourine and harp. Psalm 149:3

FATHER OF THE HEAVENLY LIGHTS

אֲבִי הַמְּאֹרֹת

Ah-vee Hahm-o-rote

Every good and perfect gift is from above,
coming down from the Father of the heavenly lights,
who does not change like shifting shadows.

James 1:17

Every good thing that happens in my life is from You.

Thank You, dear Ah-vee Hahm-o-rote,

Father of the Heavenly Lights.

Even in the trials, You bring forth good.

Thank You that You are never-changing, always loving.

There is no variation.

You are the same yesterday, today and forever.

Thank You for giving light to my path.

FATHER TO THE FATHERLESS

אֲבִי יְתוֹמִים

Ah-vee Y'to-meem

A father to the fatherless, a defender of widows,

is God in His holy dwelling.

Psalm 68:5

What promises that You make to Your own!

How You love the fatherless.

Thank You for being the Best Father. There is none like You.

It is a blessing to be Your child.

FEAR OF ISAAC

פַּחַד יִצְחָק

Fah-khad Yeets-khahk

If the God of my father, the God of Abraham
and the Fear of Isaac, had not been with me, You
would surely have sent me away empty-handed.

Genesis 31:42a

Just as Isaac had a holy fear of You, I do, too.

You, the Fear of Isaac, Fah-khad Yeets-khahk,

reign supreme.

You are to be revered, honored,

glorified, extolled, lauded.

You protect me,

You deal with my enemies.

I fear You and I love You.

FIRST AND THE LAST

רִאשׁוֹן וְאַחֲרוֹן

Ree-shone V'ah-kha-rone

I am the Alpha and the Omega,

the First and the Last,

the Beginning and the End.

Revelation 22:13

Thank You for always being there.

FIRSTBORN FROM THE DEAD

בְּכוֹר שֶׁקָם מִוֹהַמֵּתִים

V'khor Sheh-kahm Meen Hah-may-teem

And He is the head of the body, the church; He is the beginning and the firstborn

from among the dead, so that in everything He might have the supremacy.

Colossians 1:18

I glory in Your name, the Firstborn from the Dead,

the one who rose by God's power!

You are our evidence that Resurrection is ours.

How I praise Your name!

FIRSTBORN OVER ALL CREATION

וּבְכוֹר כָּל נִבְרָא

Oov-khor kol Neev-rah

He is the image of the invisible God,

the firstborn over all creation.

Colossians 1:15

Eternity is You.

Before anything was, You were, You are and You will be.

What a wonder You are! I am awed to be in Your presence.

FLESH

Bah-sahr

The word became flesh and made His dwelling among us.

John 1:14a

Thank You for coming as Flesh, Bah-sahr.

This helps me to live as You did.

You came as man, yet fully God.

I love You, God in the Flesh.

FORGIVING GOD

אֱלוֹהַּ סְלִיחוֹת

Eh-lo-hah S'lee-khote

But You are a forgiving God, gracious and compassionate,

slow to anger and abounding in love.

Nehemiah 9:17c

Your love is amazing. No one forgives like You, LORD.

You are a God who is always

ready to pardon, ready to forgive.

There is none like You!

FRIEND OF TAX COLLECTORS AND SINNERS

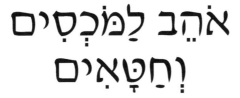

Oh-hayve Lah-mokh-seem V'kha-tah-eem

"The Son of Man came eating and drinking, and they say,
'Here is a glutton and a drunkard, a friend of tax collectors and "sinners."
But wisdom is proved right by her actions."

Matthew 11:19

Thank You, LORD, for coming to the unloved.

I know I am in good company with tax collectors and sinners.

Thank You for giving me a model to follow.

You show me how to love the unlovely.

GATE

Shah-ahr

"I am the gate; whoever enters through Me will be saved.

He will come in and go out, and find pasture."

John 10:9

You are the Only Entrance to the Father,

You are the Only Entrance to Eternal Life,

You are the Only Entrance to the Abundant Life.

How I love Your name!

"Do not swear falsely by my name and so profane the name of your God.

I am the Lord." Leviticus 19:12

GLORIOUS FATHER

אֲבִי הַכָּבוֹד

Ah-vee Hah-Kah-vode

I keep asking that the God of our Lord Yeshua HaMashiach,

the glorious Father, may give you

the Spirit of wisdom and revelation,

so that you may know Him better.

Ephesians 1:17

What glory, Glorious Father, Ah-vee Hah-Kah-vode.

You are the Best,

my eternal Father, my Glorious Father,

yet You are the Father of all.

Thank You for giving me the Spirit of wisdom and revelation,

that I may know You better.

Every day gets sweeter and sweeter with You.

GLORY OF ISRAEL

נֵצַח יִשְׂרָאֵל

Nay-tsakh Yees-rah-el

"He who is the Glory of Israel does not lie or

change His mind; for He is not a man that

He should change His mind."

1 Samuel 15:29

Such splendor befits Your name, Glory of Israel,

Nay-tsakh Yees-rah-el.

As I daily place my trust in You,

I know that I shall not be disappointed.

You may keep me waiting for a season or two,

but You are true to Your word, and not one of

Your promises has ever failed.

You are the Glory of Israel,

and You are my Glory, too.

How I love Your name!

Holy Father, protect them by the power of Your name—the

name You gave Me—so that they may be one as We are one.

John 17:11b

GOD

אֱלֹהִים

Eh-lo-heem

In the beginning God created the heavens
and the earth.

Genesis 1:1

You were Eh-lo-heem, God, in the beginning.

You are Eh-lo-heem, God, today.

You will be Eh-lo-heem, God, tomorrow.

Past, present, and future, You are God.

Help me to worship You as Your name deserves.

A multiple unity is Your name:

You are complex, yet You know even the hairs of my head.

Even though I admit that I don't understand You, I love You,

and more importantly,

I know that You love me.

GOD ALMIGHTY

אֵל שַׁדַּי

El Shad-i

When Abram was ninety-nine years old,

the LORD appeared to Him and said,

"I am GOD Almighty; walk before Me

and be blameless."

Genesis 17:1

That is my humble plea to You, God Almighty, El Shad-i:

help me to walk before You and be blameless.

With every word, with every action, with every thought, may all

I do be pleasing unto You.

How I praise Your wonderful name!

"Salvation is found in no one else, for there is no other name under heaven

given to men by which we must be saved." Acts 4:12

GOD AND SAVIOR OF ISRAEL

אֱלֹהֵי יִשְׂרָאֵל
מוֹשִׁיעַ

Eh-lo-hay Yees-rah-el Mo-shee-ah

Truly You are a God who hides Himself,

O God and Savior of Israel.

Isaiah 45:15

Thank You LORD, that even though

You hid YourSELF from Israel,

You still may be found,

O God and Savior of Israel, Eh-lo-hay Yees-rah-el Mo-shee-ah.

Even though You cannot be seen, I can see You.

with eyes of faith.

"Salvation is found in no one else, for there is no other name under heaven given to men by which we must be saved." Acts 4:12

GOD MOST HIGH

אֱלֹהִים עֶלְיוֹן

Eh-lo-heem El-yone

I cry out to God Most High,

to God, who fulfills His purpose for me.

Psalm 57:2

I cry out to You, for You hear me and

Your ear is not deaf to my cry. O God,

You know my heart cry, and only

You can fill that empty place inside.

By faith, I will wait for Your hand of deliverance,

Eh-lo-heem El-yone.

He restores my soul.

He guides me in paths of righteousness

for His name's sake.

Psalm 23:3

GOD MY MAKER

אֱלוֹהַ עֹשָׂי

Eh-lo-hah O'si

"But no one says, 'Where is God my Maker,

who gives songs in the night?' "

Job 35:10

There is no need to hide from You, for You are God my Maker,

Eh-lo-hah O-si. You made me; You fashioned me; You know

everything there is to know about me, and You love me more than

I love myself. How I praise You, dear God,

for the marvelous plan that You have for my life.

GOD MY SAVIOR

אֱלֹהֵי יִשְׁעִי

Eh-lo-hay Yeesh-ee

The LORD lives! Praise be to my Rock!

Exalted be God my Savior!

Psalm 18:46

There is none like You, O God my Savior, Eh-lo-hay Yeesh-ee.
You save me from my sinful self. Thank You for saving me from
eternal death. I desire to do Your will. How I praise You for
this wonderful plan of Yours—from before time began.
Thank You for Your abundant saving grace; thank You for all that
You have saved me from—much that I will never know.
How I praise Your name.

At that time, men began to call on
the name of the LORD.
Genesis 4:26b

GOD OF ABRAHAM

אֱלֹהֵי אַבְרָהָם

Eh-lo-hay Ahv-rah-hahm

"If the God of my father, the God of Abraham
and the Fear of Isaac, had not been with me, You
surely would have sent me away empty-handed."

Genesis 31:42a

What an example Abraham was. By faith, he believed
and it was accounted unto Him as righteousness. When
I take my eyes off You, to look at the storms, trials or
worldly temptations, help me then to remember
Abraham, and how You blessed his faith. O God of
Abraham, Eh-lo-hay Ahv-rah-hahm, help me to live out
the days of my life with the same faith that Abraham had.

GOD OF ABRAHAM, ISAAC AND JACOB

אֱלֹהֵי אַבְרָהָם
יִצְחָק וְיַעֲקֹב

Eh-lo-hay Ahv-rah-hahm Yeets-khakh V'Yah-ah-cove

"Go, assemble the elders of Israel and say to them,
'The Lord, the God of your fathers--the God of Abraham, Isaac and Jacob--appeared to me and said:
"I have watched over you and have seen what has been done to you in Egypt." ' "
Exodus 3:16

What a wonderful God You are!
You are Eh-lo-hay Ahv-rah-hahm Yeets-khakh V'Yah-ah-cove,
the God of Abraham, Isaac and Jacob,
and You are my God!
I am in good company.
Thank You, LORD!

GOD OF ALL COMFORT

אֱלֹהֵי כָּלנֶחָמָה

Eh-lo-hay Khawl Neh-kha-mah

Praise be to the God and Father of our Lord Yeshua HaMashiach (Jesus Christ),

the Father of compassion and the God of all comfort.

2 Corinthians 1:3

What a comfort to know You, the God of All Comfort.

No matter what my afflictions, Your comfort is greater.

Thank You that in the midst of a storm,

You are my peace, my Shalom,

O God of All Comfort, Eh-lo-hay Khawl Neh-kha-mah.

GOD OF ALL GRACE

אֱלֹהֵי הַחֶסֶד

Eh-lo-hay Ha-Kheh-sed

And the God of all grace,

who called you to His eternal glory in Christ,

after you have suffered a little while,

will Himself restore you and make you strong, firm and steadfast.

1 Peter 5:10

Dear God,

I know that You are waiting for me at the finish line of this trial.

As I persevere, thank You for perfecting and establishing me in

Messiah. Thank You, Eh-lo-hay Ha-Kheh-sed, for always

bringing me through victoriously.

Thank You that success is dependent not upon my strength,

but upon my reliance on Your strength and Your grace.

How lovely is Your name, O God of All Grace.

In that day you will say: "Give thanks to the LORD, call on His name;

make known among the nations what He has done,

and proclaim that His name is exalted."

Isaiah 12:4

GOD OF ALL MANKIND

אֱלֹהֵי כָּל־בָּשָׂר

Eh-lo-hay Kawl Bah-sar

"I am the Lord, the God of all mankind. Is anything too hard for Me?"

Jeremiah 32:27

How I praise You!

O Eh-lo-hay Kawl Bah-sar,

thank You that there are no limits to You.

We are but flesh, but You reign over all flesh.

How I praise You for this wonderful creation.

Thank You for Yeshua, Jesus, who came as

God in the flesh, to show me how to live.

Words cannot describe my joy in thanksgiving to You!

GOD OF ALL THE EARTH

אֱלֹהֵי כָל-הָאָרֶץ

Eh-lo-hay Khawl Ha-Arets

"For your Maker is your husband—
the Lord Almighty is His name—
the Holy One of Israel is your Redeemer;
He is called the God of all the earth."

Isaiah 54:5

How awesome it is for me to think that You,
the God of All the Earth, love me.
You, Eh-lo-hay Khawl Ha-Arets, care for the birds,
You care for the animals, and You care for me.
How I praise Your name,
for You alone are great.

GOD OF ALL THE FAMILIES OF ISRAEL

אֱלֹהִים לְכֹל מִשְׁפְּחוֹת יִשְׂרָאֵל

Eh-lo-heem l'khol Meesh-p'khot Yees-rah-el

"At that time," declares the LORD,

"I will be the God of all the clans of Israel,

and they will be My people."

Jeremiah 31:1

I get encouraged when I think of You, God,

God of All the Families of Israel, Eh-lo-heem l'khol

Meesh-p'khot Yees-rah-el, how You led all of them

through the waters of the Red Sea.

May I recall this power, when I have my next "Red Sea"

experience. You love me; You desire the best for me.

Help me to trust You, just as the families of Israel did

as they followed Your leading through the Red Sea.

Men will hear of Your great name and Your mighty hand

and Your outstretched arm. 1 Kings 8:42a

GOD OF DANIEL

אֱלָהֵהּ דִּי-דָנִיֵּאל

Eh-lo-hay Dee Dah-nee-el

"I issue a decree that in every part of my kingdom
people must fear and reverence the
God of Daniel."

Daniel 6:26

Thank You, LORD, that regardless of the trial in which
I find myself, You are always there to deliver, O God of
Daniel, Eh-lo-hay Dee Dah-nee-el. As Daniel found Himself
in the lions' den, he looked up, and You closed the lions'
mouths. You are the Mighty One; You gave Daniel favor and
You give me favor, not because of me, but because of Thee.
How I praise You.

GOD OF ELIJAH

אֱלֹהֵי אֵלִיָּהוּ

Eh-lo-hay Ay-lee-yah-hoo

Then he took the cloak that had fallen from him and struck the
water with it. "Where now is the LORD, the God of Elijah?"
he asked.
When he struck the water, it divided to the right and to the left,
and he crossed over.

2 Kings 2:14

You did great and mighty things through Elijah. You even split
the waters through his hands. You are a mighty God, and I praise
You for Your mighty works through men and women of God. Will
You use me as You used Elijah?

GOD OF GLORY

El-HaKavode

The voice of the LORD is over the waters;

the God of glory thunders.

Psalm 29:3a

Dear Father,

The fear to approach You does not exist any more, for Yeshua

Jesus made access to Your glory available, through His death on the cross.

God of Glory, El-HaKavode, whose face is so holy one

cannot look upon it, how I praise You. There is no one higher,

more lofty, more regal, more wonderful, than You.

Your glory is all supreme, all sovereign, and all holy.

How I love Your name!

Sing the glory of His name; make His praise glorious! Psalm 66:2

GOD of gods

Eh-lo-hay Ha-Eh-lo-heem

For the LORD your God is God of gods.

Deuteronomy 10:17a

Dear God,

Help me to have no other gods but You. You are

God of gods, all powerful, supreme and sovereign.

Nothing else in this world is important to me but You.

How I praise You for Your wonderful "keeping" power,

for truly You keep me in love with You,

God of gods, Eh-lo-hay Ha-Eh-lo-heem.

I love Your name.

GOD OF HEAVEN

Eh-lo-hay HaShah-My-eem

"This is what Cyrus king of Persia says,
'The LORD, the God of heaven, has given me all
the kingdoms of the earth.' "

2 Chronicles 36:23a

May I always remember that Your view of me means
everything—Your view is from above, O God of Heaven,
Eh-lo-hay HaShah-My-eem.
How I praise You for seeing me through every challenge, trial
and test. Your view is omniscient, and may I nevermore get
stymied by what I see here—for it is a finite microscopic view.
Give me faith to trust You, O God of Heaven.

Therefore go and make disciples of all nations, baptizing them in the
name of the Father and of the Son and of the Holy Spirit.

Matthew 28:19

GOD OF HEAVEN AND GOD OF THE EARTH

אֱלֹהֵי
הַשָּׁמַיִם
וֵאלֹהֵי הָאָרֶץ

Eh-lo-hay Hah-shah-My-eem Vay-lo-hay Hah-ah-rets

"I want you to swear by the LORD,

the God of heaven and the God of earth,

that you will not get a wife for my son

from the daughters of the Canaanites, among whom I am living."

Genesis 24:3

What a miracle it is that You know me, God of Heaven

and God of the Earth, Eh-lo-hay Hah-shah-My-eem Vay-lo-hay Hah-ah-rets.

Even though You are in heaven, You are mindful of me on earth.

What a glorious mystery!

GOD OF HOSTS

אֱלֹהִים צְבָאוֹת

Eh-lo-heem Ts'vah-ote

Restore us, O God of hosts;

Cause Your face to shine,

And we shall be saved!

Psalm 80:7 NKJV

O God of Hosts, Eh-lo-heem Ts'vah-ote,

God of the Hosts, God of the armies of heaven,

thank You that the power of Your might goes

before me in battle.

You surround me with the hosts of heaven and

armies of heaven to help me.

Thank You that as I yield myself to You,

Your strength is around me.

Help me to go through the day ever aware that

You, the God of Hosts, the God of the armies of heaven,

are with me.

GOD OF ISAAC

אֱלֹהֵי יִצְחָק

Eh-lo-hay Yeets-khahk

There above it stood the LORD, and He said:
"I am the LORD, the God of your father Abraham
and the God of Isaac."

Genesis 28:13a

When I think of Isaac, innocently laying himself down when
his father Abraham took Him to Mount Moriah, I wonder how
he could do that. And yet You were there, God of Isaac,
Eh-lo-hay Yeets-khahk.

I want to be like Isaac, willingly able to lay myself down before the
Father, fully trusting You, knowing that Father knows best.
In You I trust, O God, and I know that I will never be ashamed.
How I adore Your name.

GOD OF ISRAEL

אֱלֹהֵי
יִשְׂרָאֵל

Eh-lo-hay Yis-ra-el

So the multitude marveled when they saw the mute speaking,

the maimed made whole,

the lame walking,

and the blind seeing;

and they glorified the God of Israel.

Matthew 15:31

You, the God of Israel, Eh-lo-hay Yis-ra-el, are

the same yesterday, today and forever.

Thank You for Your divine guidance in my life,

O God of Israel.

You that keep Israel (and me) never slumber or sleep.

What a comfort You are!

GOD OF JACOB

Eh-lo-hay Yah-ah-kove

May the Lord answer you when you are in distress;

may the name of the God of Jacob protect you.

Psalm 20:1

There is only One who knows my thoughts,

who hears my heart,

who can answer my prayers.

The same God who led Jacob is the same God who leads me.

There is much comfort in knowing You,

Eh-lo-hay Yah-ah-kove.

GOD OF JUSTICE

Eh-lo-hay Meesh-paht

For the LORD is a God of justice.
Blessed are all who wait for Him!
Isaiah 30:18b

If I try to judge matters with my limited vision, I often
come up short. But if I place my vision on You, and
look to You, O God of Justice, Eh-lo-hay Meesh-paht,
You always come forth with the right answer—always!
What a peace there is in knowing that Your ways are
perfect, and that if I rest in Your will, Perfect Justice
will always be the outcome.
What an awesome God You are.

You have exalted above all things Your name and Your word.
Psalm 138:2b

GOD OF LOVE AND PEACE

אֱלֹהֵי הָאַהֲבָה וְהַשָׁלוֹם

Eh-lo-hay Ha-ah-ha-vah V'ha-sha-lom

Finally, brothers, goodby.

Aim for perfection, listen to my appeal,

be of one mind, live in peace.

And the God of love and peace will be with you.

2 Corinthians 13:11

Love and Peace—two wonderful attributes of You, LORD.

Thank You!

Thank You that Your love is not dependent upon my right deeds or

my right living, but it is based on You and Your love for me.

How I praise Your name, Eh-lo-hay Ha-ah-ha-vah V'ha-sha-lom.

GOD OF MY FATHER

Eh-lo-hay Ah-vee

"I see that Your father's attitude toward me is not what it was before,

but the God of my father has been with me."

Genesis 31:5

How grateful I am for the assurance of

Your presence with me.

I need not worry about the future, or others'

opinions of me, for I know that

You will be with me.

Thank You, Eh-lo-hay Ah-vee, the God of my Father.

Through You we push back our enemies;

through Your name we trample our foes.

Psalm 44:5

GOD OF MY LIFE

אֵל חַיָּי

El Khi-i

By day the LORD directs His love,
at night His song is with me—a prayer
to the God of my life.
Psalm 42:8

You are the God of my Life, El Khi-i. There is such
a peace to know that You are the author of my life's story.
Through hard times and good times, You have been there
with me. For every chapter in my life, You have been
there, dear LORD. What a blessing to know that You
are the boss of my life, You are God to me. Help me to
walk humbly as Your servant, with the light of Your word
guiding my every step.

GOD OF MY PRAISE

אֱלֹהֵי
תְהִלָּתִי

Eh-lo-hay T'hee-lah-tee

Do not keep silent,

O GOD OF MY PRAISE!

Psalm 109:1

O God, how I praise You for the answers that

You give to my prayers.

Sometimes, yes, there is silence, and I want to ask why.

At these times, help me to hang on to Your every promise,

and help me believe in my heart that

You will never leave me,

You will never forsake me,

and You will answer my prayers.

I will wait on You, Eh-lo-hay T'hee-lah-tee.

Yes, in the way of Your judgments,

O LORD, we have waited for You;

the desire of our soul is for Your name

and for the remembrance of You. Isaiah 26:8 NKJV

GOD OF MY RIGHTEOUSNESS

Eh-lo-hay Tseed-kee

Hear me when I call, O GOD OF MY RIGHTEOUSNESS!

You have relieved me in my distress;

Have mercy on me, and hear my prayer.

Psalm 4:1 NKJV

O God,

my righteousness is all because of Yeshua, Jesus living in my heart.

Messiah in me, the Hope of Glory, is the praise on my mouth today.

For God made Messiah, who knew no sin, to be sin for us, that we

might become the righteousness of God in Messiah.

O Eh-lo-hay Tseed-kee,

how I praise You for the bounty of blessings that You give!

GOD OF PEACE

אֱלֹהֵי
הַשָּׁלוֹם

Eh-lo-hay Ha-Sha-lom

The God of peace will soon crush Satan under your feet.

Romans 16:20a

You are the God of Peace, Eh-lo-hay Ha-Sha-lom.

Yet I thank You because You go to battle for me.

How glad I am that I need not trust in my hands,

my ability or my strength for defense.

I simply put my life into Your hands

and have all the help I need.

How I praise You!

GOD OF THE HEBREWS

אֱלֹהֵי
הָעִבְרִיִּים

Eh-lo-hay Ha-eev-ree-yeem

Then they said, "The God of the Hebrews has met with us."

Exodus 5:3a

Thank You, LORD, that Your plan included the Hebrews.

From them came the Messiah.

Thank You for this marvelous legacy.

I do not claim to fully understand Your plan, but I thank You for it.

GOD OF THE JEWS

אֱלֹהִים לַיְּהוּדִים

Eh-lo-heem L-Y'hoo-deem

Is God the God of Jews only?

Romans 3:29

I thank You, wonderful God, that You are God of everybody,
whether they know it or not. I praise Your wonderful name,
God of the Jews, Hah-Eh-lo-heem L-Y'hoo-deem, that
You are God of the Jews, God of the Non-Jews.
I am just glad that I know Your name.

Although our sins testify against us, O LORD, do something for
the sake of Your name. Jeremiah 14:7a

GOD OF THE SPIRITS OF ALL MANKIND

אֱלֹהֵי הָרוּחֹת לְכָל־בָּשָׂר

Eh-lo-hay Ha-roo-kote L-khol Bah-sahr

"May the LORD,

the God of the spirits of all mankind,

appoint a man over this community."

Numbers 27:16

God of the Spirits of all Mankind,

Eh-lo-hay Ha-roo-kote L-khol Bah-sahr,

You are beyond words.

You are beyond my intelligence to grasp any understanding of You.

Yet I love You and praise You for Your magnificent plan that

You have for my life, and all the others who know You.

GOD OF TRUTH

Ayl Eh-meht

Into Your hands I commit my spirit;

redeem me, O LORD, the God of truth.

Psalm 31:5

To know You, God of Truth, gives me much peace.

In this world where many are searching for truth,

how blessed I am to know You,

Ayl Eh-meht, God of Truth!

GOD, THE LORD, THE STRENGTH OF MY SALVATION

יְהוִה
אֲדֹנָי עֹז
יְשׁוּעָתִי

A-do-ni A-do-ni Oz Y'shu-a-tee

"O GOD the Lord, the strength of my salvation,
You have covered my head in the day of battle."

Psalm 140:7 NKJV

O LORD, You give me the strength to work out

my own salvation, with fear and trembling.

I look to You for help.

Some days seem so hard, but all

You ask me to do is to rest in You,

for You are the Strength of my Salvation,

A-do-ni A-do-ni Oz Y'shu-a-tee.

Thank You for Your help,

Your hand of deliverance.

GOD WHO FORGIVES

אֵל נֹשֵׂא

El No-say

You answered them, O LORD our God;

You were to them God-Who-Forgives,

though You took vengeance on their deeds.

Psalm 99:8 NKJV

O LORD, how many times a day are You

God-Who-Forgives.

How I thank You for Your never-failing love,

Your lovingkindness O El No-say,

God-Who-Forgives.

May I live this day with a humble heart,

knowing that my goodness is not of me

but of Thee; my sinfulness is of me, but

because of Thee, I am forgiven.

Turn to me and have mercy on me,

as You always do to those who love Your name.

Psalm 119:132

GOD WHO PERFORMS MIRACLES

אֵל עֹשֵׂה פֶּלֶא

El Oh-seh Feh-leh

You are the God who performs miracles;

You display Your power among the peoples.

Psalm 77:14

What a wonderful name to be known by,

God Who Performs Miracles, El O-seh Peh-leh.

Every day, how I thank You for performing

these miracles for me—an unexpected letter,

a surprise check in the mail,

a "serendipitous" meeting—

none were happenstance; they were all done by

a loving God who wishes to remain anonymous.

What a blessing to have You guide my life.

I will bow down toward Your holy temple and will praise Your

name for Your love and Your faithfulness.

Psalm 138:2a

GOD WHO SAVES ME

אֱלֹהֵי תְּשׁוּעָתִי

Eh-lo-hay T'shu-a-tee

Save me from bloodguilt, O God,

the God who saves me,

and my tongue will sing of Your righteousness.

Psalm 51:14

In thought, word, or deed, I have erred in Your sight.

I thank You that You are the God of my salvation,

Eh-lo-hay T'shu-a-tee, the God Who Saves Me.

Thank You for the Blood of the Lamb that cleanses me from

all of my sins, and allows me access to Your wide throne of grace.

O LORD, You are my God;

I will exalt You and praise Your name,

for in perfect faithfulness

You have done marvelous things,

things planned long ago.

Isaiah 25:1

GOOD

Tove

The LORD is good,
a refuge in times of trouble.
Nahum 1:7a

You are Good, Tove.
You are the ultimate refuge,
The One to run to in times of trouble.
You know who are Yours.
I bless Your name.

O LORD, You are my God;
I will exalt You and praise Your name,
for in perfect faithfulness
You have done marvelous things,
things planned long ago.
Isaiah 25:1

GOOD TEACHER, GOOD RABBI

Rah-bee Ha-Tov

As Yeshua Jesus started on his way, a man ran up
to Him and fell on his knees before Him. "Good teacher,"
he asked, "what must I do to inherit eternal life?"
Mark 10:17

Thank You, LORD, for being my Good Teacher, my Rah-bee
Ha-Tov. You have all the patience in the world; You have
all the wisdom in the world—You know it all, and I thank You,
for Your teaching is perfect. Thank You that I never graduate
until I see You face to face. How I praise Your name!

GREAT

Gah-dole

"How great You are, O Sovereign LORD!

There is no one like You,

and there is no God but You, as we have heard with our own ears."

2 Samuel 7:22

Great are You, Gah-dole!

You reign on high; there is no one like You!

You do mighty things:

You save.

You heal.

You care.

You love.

You are great!

GREAT AND AWESOME GOD

אֵל
הַגָּדוֹל
וְהַנּוֹרָא

El Hah-gah-dol V'hah-no-rah

"O LORD, God of heaven, the great and awesome God,
who keeps His covenant of love with those who love
Him and obey His commands, let Your ear be attentive
and Your eyes open to hear the prayer Your servant
is praying before You."

Nehemiah 1:5-6a

Our finite words can hardly come close to praising You,
the Great and Awesome God, El Hah-gah-dol V'han-no-rah.
You are holy, You are wonderful, You are great,
You are awesome. When I think of all of the wonderful
things that You have done for me, and then I multiply
that times all the people in the world—
well, God, You are Awesome.
And what a wonder You are!

Let every creature praise His holy name for ever and ever.

Psalm 145:21b

GREAT HIGH PRIEST

כֹּהֵן גָּדוֹל
נַעֲלֶה
עַד־מְאֹד

Ko-hayn Gah-dole Nah-ah-leh Ahd M'ode

Therefore, since we have a great high priest

who has gone through the heavens,

Yeshua Jesus the Son of God,

let us hold firmly to the faith we profess.

Hebrews 4:14

You sent Yeshua Jesus to be my Great High Priest,

to intercede for me,

as I am unworthy to come before You.

But because He lives to intercede for me,

I can now come into Your presence with joy,

face to face and unashamed!

GREAT KING

מֶלֶךְ רָב

Meh-lekh Rahv

"But I tell you, Do not swear at all: either by heaven,
for it is God's throne; or by the earth, for it is His footstool,
or by Jerusalem, for it is the city of the Great King."
Matthew 5:34-35

LORD,
How much You love Jerusalem, as it is Your city, the
city of the Great King, Meh-lekh Rahv. You are my Great King,
and You are sovereign over any other ruler, principality
or authority in my life. Thank You for Your divine sovereign rule.
How I praise Your wonderful name.

GREAT SHEPHERD OF THE SHEEP

רֹעֵה
הַצֹּאן
הַגָּדוֹל

Ro-ayh Hah-tson Hah-gah-dol

May the God of peace, who through the blood of the
eternal covenant brought back from the dead our Lord
Jesus, that great Shepherd of the sheep, equip you
with everything good for doing His will.
Hebrews 13:20-21a

Father,

How thankful I am for the Great Shepherd. Sometimes I just
want to say "Bah, Bah, Baaaaaaaaaah" when I don't know
what to do. When I realize that You have everything under control,
I don't need to worry about a thing. How I love Your name,
Great Shepherd of the Sheep, Ro-ayh Hah-tson Hah-gah-dol.

You are among us, O LORD, and we bear Your name;
do not forsake us! Jeremiah 14:9b

GUIDE OF MY YouTH

אַלּוּף
נְעֻרַי

Ah-loof N'oo-ri

Will you not from this time cry to Me,

"My Father, You are the guide of my Youth"?

Jeremiah 3:4 NKJV

When my heart is overwhelmed and I have nowhere else
to go, I run to You, Ah-loof N'oo-ri, Guide of my Youth.
You know my ways; You will lead me on level paths.
How I praise Your name!

For Your name's sake, O LORD, preserve my life;
in Your righteousness, bring me out of trouble.

Psalm 143:11

HE WHO FIGHTS FOR YOU

Hoo Hah-neel-khahm Lah-khem

"One man of you shall chase a thousand,
for the LORD Your God is He who fights for you,
as He promised you."
Joshua 23:10 NKJV

What a comfort it is to know that when I go to battle,
You fight for me.
Hoo Hah-neel-khahm Lah-khem. You are
He Who Fights for You.
What a blessing to be on Your side!

HEAD OF THE BODY

Rosh Hah-ay-dah

And He is the head of the body, the church; He is the
beginning and the firstborn from among the dead, so that
in everything He might have the supremacy.

Colossians 1:18

We, Your children, are so blessed that You are the Head
of the Body, Rosh Hah-ay-dah. You are the head of the
assembly of believers; You have gone before us; You chart
the path. Thank You for loving the Body so much that You
gave Your all. Help us to give our all for You.

HEAD OF THE CHURCH

Rosh Ha-ay-dah

For the husband is the head of the wife as

Christ is the head of the church,

His body, of which He is the Savior.

Ephesians 5:23

Yeshua, thank You that You are the Head of the Church.

The Church is Your body here on earth.

Help us to be Your arms and hands and feet to serve each other.

Your name is wonderful.

HEAD OVER EVERY POWER AND AUTHORITY

רֹאשׁ
לְכָלמִשְׂרָה
וְשִׂלְטוֹן

Rosh L'kol Mees-rah V'Sheel-tone

. . . and you have been given fullness in Christ Messiah,
Who is the head over every power and authority.
Colossians 2:10

Thank You, LORD, that regardless of any regime or principality in power,
You are still sovereign over all.
Thank You that truly all power comes from You.
I shall not fear but live, and declare Your marvelous works!

HEIR OF ALL THINGS

בַּעַל
נַחֲלָה
בַּכֹּל

Vah-ahl Nah-kha-lah Vah-kole

But in these last days He has spoken to us by His Son,
whom He appointed heir of all things, and through whom He made the universe.

Hebrews 1:2

You are God's Son, the Divine Son,

the One who inherits all things from the Father.

Sometimes it is such a mystery for me to comprehend,

yet I praise Your glorious name!

HIGH PRIEST

הַכֹּהֵן
הַגָּדוֹל

Hah Ko-hayn HaGah-dol

Therefore, holy brothers, who share in the heavenly
calling, fix Your thoughts on Yeshua, Jesus, the apostle
and high priest whom we confess.

Hebrews 3:1

May I have eyes for no one else but the One who gives me
life. You who laid Your life down for me, serve as a Priest
forever. All other priests die, but You live forever, eternally,
to intercede for me. You were the Gift and the Giver; what
a wonder You are, High Priest, Hah Ko-hayn HaGah-dol.

HIS ANOINTED ONE

M'shee-kho

The kings of the earth take their stand and

the rulers gather together against

the Lord and against His Anointed One.

Acts 4:26

Some day, we will all look into the face of Yeshua,

God's Anointed One. What a marvelous sight that will be.

His Anointed One is the long awaited Messiah!

HIS HOLY ONE

K'do-sho

So the Light of Israel will be for a fire, and His Holy One for a flame;
it will burn and devour his thorns and his briers in one day.
Isaiah 10:17 NKJV

What a blessing to know Yeshua, His Holy One, K'do-sho.
You light up my life with the flame of Your love.

Glory in His holy name; let the hearts of
those who seek the LORD rejoice.
1 Chronicles 16:10

HIS INDESCRIBABLE GIFT

מַתָּן

עָצוּם

מִסַּפֵּר

Mah-tahn Ah-tsoom Mee-sah-pare

Thanks be to God for His indescribable gift!

2 Corinthians 9:15

You are better than any gift man can give. You are the gift of life,

eternal life; You are the giver of life. You are the

Indescribable Gift! No words can fully describe just how wonderful

You truly are! How I praise Your name.

HIS MAKER

O'say-hoo

"Israel has forgotten his Maker..."

Hosea 8:14a

Israel forgot his Maker, O'say-hoo.

Help me never to forget You.

HOLY

Kah-dosh

Let them praise Your great and
awesome name—He is holy.

Psalm 99:3

Everything about You is holy and
righteous and pure. Your name is Holy.
Your nature is Holy. Kadosh, Kadosh,
Kadosh: Holy, Holy, Holy,
May Your holy name always
be close to my heart.

HOLY AND RIGHTEOUS ONE

קָדוֹשׁ
וְצַדִּיק

Kah-dosh V'tza-deek

"You disowned the Holy and Righteous One
and asked that a murderer be released to you."

Acts 3:14

Even as Your enemies cursed You,

You returned love towards them.

Your character is holy and righteous.

I love You, Holy and Righteous One.

HOLY ONE OF GOD

קְדוֹשׁ
הָאֱלֹהִים

K'Dosh Hah-Eh-lo-heem

"Ha! What do You want with us, Yeshua Jesus of
Nazareth? Have You come to destroy us? I know
who You are—the Holy One of God!"

Luke 4:34

Sometimes I am really amazed that so many people
know who You are, but they really don't know You.
Thank You that I know You as the Holy One of God,
K'dosh Hah-Eh-lo-heem. I thank You that I can approach
You and be honest with You, and You won't turn me away,
because You love me.
Thank You for Your boundless love.

But I have raised you up for this very purpose, that I might show
you My power and that My name might be proclaimed in all the earth.

Exodus 9:16

HOLY ONE OF ISRAEL

K'dosh Yis-ra-el

For I am the LORD, Your God,

the Holy One of Israel, Your Savior.

Isaiah 43:3a

Father, may I never be put into a position to tempt You,

K'dosh Yis-ra-el, Holy One of Israel.

May I only seek to do Your will.

You are Holy and I cannot look upon You,

except by the blood of the sinless

Seh Ha Eloheem, the Lamb of God.

What a gift You have given,

O Holy One of Israel.

Glory in His holy name;

let the hearts of those who seek the LORD rejoice.

1 Chronicles 16:10

HOPE OF ISRAEL

מִקְוֵה
יִשְׂרָאֵל

Meek-vay Yis-ra-el

O LORD, the hope of Israel,

all who forsake You will be put to shame.

Jeremiah 17:13a

You are my Hope, O Meek-vay Yis-ra-el.

my sorrow may endure for the evening, but

joy comes in the morning.

You are my Hope.

When all else fails, there is You.

Help me never to give up on

Your wonderful name.

HOPE OF THEIR FATHERS

מִקְוֵה
אֲבוֹתֵיהֶם

Meek-vay Ah-vo-tay-hem

Whoever found them devoured them; their
enemies said, "We are not guilty, for they
sinned against the LORD, their true pasture,
the LORD, hope of their fathers."

Jeremiah 50:7

Pagan logic is always wrong, because it is never
fixed on You, the Living Word. You were
Meek-vay Ah-vo-tay-hem, Hope of Their Fathers.
You are that name today. How I love Your name.

HORN OF MY SALVATION

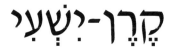

Keh-rehn Yeesh-ee

He is my shield and the horn
of my salvation, my stronghold.
Psalm 18:2b

When I am afraid, I shall run to You and grab hold of You,
Horn of my Salvation, Keh-rehn Yeesh-ee.
You will protect me; how I praise Your name.

I AM HE

אֲנִי הוּא

Ah-nee hoo

"I am," said Jesus.

Mark 14:62

"I am He," the most powerful way to identify YourSELF.

From eternity to eternity, You are God.

I AM THE FIRST AND I AM THE LAST

אֲנִי רִאשׁוֹן וַאֲנִי אַחֲרוֹן

Ah-nee Ree-shon va-Ah-nee Ah-kha-ron

"This is what the LORD says—

Israel's King and Redeemer, the LORD Almighty:

I am the first and I am the last;

apart from me there is no God."

Isaiah 44:6

You set the heavens and the earth in motion with
one stretch of Your hand. You will be when no one
else will be. You said, "I Am the First and I Am the
Last, Ah-nee Ree-shon va-Ah-nee Ah-kha-ron."
As long as I am YourS, I need not be concerned
with anything else. Your name says it all.

I AM WHO I AM

Eh-yeh Ah-sher Eh-yeh

God said to Moses,

"I AM WHO I AM.

This is what you are to say to the Israelites:

'I AM has sent me to you.' "

Exodus 3:14

You are timeless. How grateful I am to know that

You hold all the keys to the Kingdom.

Today I rest in knowing You, the Great I AM,

Eh-yeh Ah-sher Eh-yeh.

You are the same, yesterday, today and forever.

What peace that brings to my soul.

IMAGE OF GOD

Tseh-lehm Ha-Eh-lo-heem

The god of this age has blinded the minds of unbelievers,

so that they cannot see the light of the

gospel of the glory of Christ, who is the image of God.

2 Corinthians 4:4

Better than any photograph image, Yeshua,

You are the exact Image of God.

What a marvelous mystery God has unveiled in You:

perfect God and perfect man.

Then all the peoples on earth will see that

You are called by the name of the LORD,

and they will fear You. Deuteronomy 28:10

IMAGE OF THE INVISIBLE GOD

צֶלֶם

אֱלֹהִים

אֲשֶׁר פָּנָיו

לֹא יֶרְאוּ

Tseh-lehm Eh-lo-heem Ah-share
Pah-nav Lo Yay-rah-oo

He is the image of the invisible God,

the firstborn over all creation.

Colossians 1:15

You are the Image of the God who cannot be seen,

whose countenance man is unable to see.

Yet we see You by faith, and You are beautiful.

For the sake of His great name the LORD

will not reject His people,

because the LORD was pleased to make you His own. 1 Samuel 12:22

IMMANUEL

עִמָּנוּ אֵל

Ee-ma-noo Ayl

Therefore the Lord Himself will give you a sign:

The virgin will be with child and will give birth to a son,

and will call Him Immanuel.

Isaiah 7:14

Immanuel, God With Us.

God, You never forsake us.

God, You are never not with us.

Thank You for Your marvelous plan, and that

I can always know Immanuel, God With Us.

IMMORTAL

שֹׁכֵן עַד

Sho-khan Ahd

Now to the King eternal, immortal, invisible, the only God,

be honor and glory for ever and ever. Amen.

1 Timothy 1:17

Immortality fits You.

No beginning, no ending, always and forever.

What a comfort it is to know that You know me,

and that I will be with You

for eternity!

INVISIBLE

אֲשֶׁר עַיִן
לֹא
תְשׁוּרֶנּוּ

Ah-share Ayin Lo T'shoo-reh-noo

Now to the King eternal, immortal, invisible,

the only God, be honor and glory

for ever and ever. Amen.

1 Timothy 1:17

How amazing it is to know that You cannot be seen by the human eye,

yet You are everywhere, and my spirit bears witness with Your Spirit that

You are my Heavenly Father, Invisible yet always loving!

David said to the Philistine,

"You come against me with sword and spear and javelin,

but I come against you in the name of the LORD Almighty,

the God of the armies of Israel, whom You have defied." 1 Samuel 17:45

ISRAEL'S CREATOR

בּוֹרֵא
יִשְׂרָאֵל

Bo-ray Yis-rah-el

"I am the LORD, your Holy One, Israel's Creator, your King."
Isaiah 43:15

Father,

Thank You for the wonderful plan that You set into motion before time began. Thank You for being Israel's Creator, Bo-ray Yis-rah-el, and thank You for the mysterious wonder of Israel. You have kept that tiny country alive all these thousands of years. You are a truly marvelous God.

"You have persevered and have endured hardships for My name, and have not grown weary." Revelation 2:3

ISRAEL'S KING AND REDEEMER

Meh-lekh Yis-rah-el V'Go-ah-lo

"This is what the LORD says—

Israel's King and Redeemer, the LORD Almighty:

I am the first and I am the last;

apart from me there is no God."

Isaiah 44:6

Father,

How blessed I am to be redeemed by Your right hand.

Thank You that I know You, Israel's King and Redeemer,

Meh-lekh Yis-rah-el V'Go-ah-lo. You are God, and how

much more blessed am I to know that You know me.

How I love Your name.

JACOB'S KING

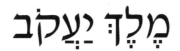

Meh-lekh Yah-ah-cove

"Present your case," says the Lord.

"Set forth your arguments," says Jacob's King.

Isaiah 41:21

It is amazing to think that the King of Jacob is also my King.

What a marvelous sovereign King You are!

When the queen of Sheba heard about the fame

of Solomon and his relation to the name of the LORD,

she came to test him with hard questions. 1 Kings 10:1

JEALOUS

Kah-nah

Do not worship any other god,
for the LORD, whose name is Jealous, is a jealous God.
Exodus 34:14

Father,
Help me to discipline my eyes and my whole being
to desire no other gods but You.
I desire to worship the Creator and not the creature.
There is no other name but Yours,
Kah-nah, Jealous God.

JESUS YESHUA OF NAZARETH

יֵשׁוּעַ הַנָּצְרִי

Yay-shoo-ah Hah-Nahtz-ree

Pilate had a notice prepared and fastened to the cross.

It read:

Jesus of Nazareth,

the King of the Jews.

John 19:19

Pilate, who longed to know truth, condemned Truth to die.

Thank You, Jesus of Nazareth, for dying in my place.

Ascribe to the LORD the glory due His name.

Bring an offering and come before Him;

worship the LORD in the splendor of His holiness.

1 Chronicles 16:29

JESUS YESHUA THE MESSIAH

יֵשׁוּעַ
הַמָּשִׁיחַ

Yay-shoo-ah Ha-Mah-Shee-akh

For the law was given through Moses; grace and
truth came through Jesus Christ.

John 1:17

The name that was so forbidden to me is now my everything.
Jesus Christ, Jesus the Messiah, my Messiah. How I love You.

JESUS YESHUA THE MESSIAH
OF NAZARETH

יֵשׁוּעַ
הַמָּשִׁיחַ
הַנָּצְרִי

Yeh-shoo-ah Hah-Mah-Shee-akh Hah-Nahtz-ree

"Then know this, you and all the people of Israel:
It is by the name of Jesus Christ of Nazareth,
whom you crucified but whom God raised from the dead,
that this man stands before You healed."

Acts 4:10

You grew up in a little tiny town in Israel. You can relate to my simple life.
Thank You for revealing Yourself to me, that I may know You,
Yeshua Jesus the Messiah of Nazareth.

Glory in His holy name; let the hearts
of those who seek the LORD rejoice.

1 Chronicles 16:10

JESUS YESHUA THE MESSIAH
OUR SAVIOR

יֵשׁוּעַ
הַמָּשִׁיחַ
מוֹשִׁיעֵנוּ

Yay-shoo-ah Hah-Mah-shee-akh Mo-shee-ay-noo

He saved us through the washing of rebirth and renewal

by the Holy Spirit,

whom He poured out on us generously

through Jesus Christ our Savior.

Titus 3:5b-6

If I had needed a doctor, You would have sent me a doctor.

If I had needed a lawyer, You would have sent me a lawyer.

But You knew I needed a Savior, so You sent me Jesus.

Oh, what a wonderful Gift!

JESUS YESHUA THE SON OF GOD

יֵשׁוּעַ בֶּן
אֱלֹהִים

Yay-sho-ah Ben Eh-lo-heem

Therefore, since we have a great high priest

who has gone through the heavens,

Jesus the Son of God,

let us hold firmly to the faith we profess.

Hebrews 4:14

Only those of us who know You can proclaim You "Son of God."

Thank You for revealing Yourself to me.

What a wonder You are!

JUDGE

Sho-fate

"Let the LORD, the Judge, decide the dispute this day
between the Israelites and the Ammonites."
Judges 11:27b

You are the only Judge I want to settle my disputes. No earthly judge
can compare to You. You judge rightly, and I praise Your name!

JUDGE OF THE EARTH

שֹׁפֵט כָּל-הָאָרֶץ

Sho-fayt Kol Hah-ah-rehts

"Far be it from you to do such a thing—to kill the
righteous with the wicked, treating the righteous
and the wicked alike. Far be it from you!
Will not the Judge of all the earth do right?"

Genesis 18:25

With all of the craziness in the world today, it is so comforting
to know that there is One who judges with righteous
judgment, the Judge of All the Earth, Sho-fayt Kol
Hah-ah-rehts. I am so thankful for Your long-suffering
nature and Your lovingkindness. Thank You for Your
judgment that is always right.

I will sacrifice a thank offering to You
and call on the name of the LORD. Psalm 116:17

JUDGE OF THE EARTH

שֹׁפֵט הָאָרֶץ

Sho-fate Hah-ah-rehtz

Rise up, O Judge of the earth;
pay back to the proud what they deserve.

Psalm 94:2

Father, when I am disappointed and crushed

because of the adversary, help me to

realize that You are the Judge of the Earth,

and You will avenge me of the enemy of my soul.

I love You.

Thank You for loving me.

JUDGE OF THE LIVING AND THE DEAD

שֹׁפֵט
הַחַיִּים
וְהַמֵּתִים

Sho-fayt Hah-khy-eem V'Hah-may-teem

"He commanded us to preach to the people and to
testify that He is the one whom God appointed as judge
of the living and the dead."

Acts 10:42

What a wonderful thing it is to know that You are the same
judge for me, whether I am living or dead. You are divine,
You are holy, You are the Judge of the Living and the Dead,
Sho-fayt Hah-khy-eem V'Hah-may-teem. What a comfort it is
to know that You will be with me always.

KING

מֶלֶךְ

Meh-lekh

The LORD is King for ever and ever;
the nations will perish from His land.
Psalm 10:16

It is good to know that there is no other king
higher than our Meh-lekh, our King.
In the daily battles of life, if we know the King,
we will have victory.
O LORD,
how I thank You that I need never worry about
the battles in my life.
You will always gain the victory.
How blessed I am to be a King's kid!

KING ETERNAL

מֶלֶךְ עוֹלָם

Meh-lekh O-lahm

Now to the King eternal, immortal, invisible,

the only God,

be honor and glory for ever and ever.

Amen.

1 Timothy 1:17

How thankful I am to know You, King Eternal.

Meh-lekh O-lahm.

Even though You are invisible,

You are nearer to me than my own breath.

May I live this day in total thankfulness.

May I live this day with a sense of Your closeness.

I love You, dear LORD.

And everyone who calls on the name of the LORD will be saved. Joel 2:32a

KING OF ALL THE EARTH

מֶלֶךְ כָּל-הָאָרֶץ

Meh-lekh Kol Hah-ah-rets

For God is the King of all the earth;

sing to Him a psalm of praise.

Psalm 47:7

What a comfort it is to know that You reign supreme

above all governing powers, all spiritual powers:

King of All the Earth, Meh-lekh Kol Hah-ah-rets.

It is wonderful to know that You have the final say.

There is peace in any storm, because You rule over

the storm, and You always bring me through.

How great is Your name!

KING OF GLORY

מֶלֶךְ הַכָּבוֹד

Meh-lekh Ha-Ka-vode

Lift up your heads, o you gates;
be lifted up, you ancient doors,
that the king of glory may come in.
Who is this King of glory?
The LORD strong and mighty,
the LORD mighty in battle.
Psalm 24:7-8

You are the King of Glory, the Meh-lekh Ha-Ka-vode.
The King of Royal Esteem, Majesty and
Abundance.
LORD, how I thank You for the glory, the
Ka-vode, of Your name.
May I so live as to bring honor to the King.

KING OF HEAVEN

מֶלֶךְ שְׁמַיָּא

Meh-lekh Sh'My-yah

Now I, Nebuchadnezzar, praise and exalt and glorify
the King of heaven, because everything He does is
right and all His ways are just.

Daniel 4:37a

What a peace it is to know that You are King of Heaven,
Meh-lekh Sh'My-yah. You will be with me in eternity,
You are with me now, and You have been with me in the past.

When I think of death, there is great peace in knowing that
You will be waiting for me in Heaven. Yes, it will be
wonderful to see Abraham, Moses, Elijah, and Paul,
but O LORD, You, the King of Heaven,
are who I desire to see the most.

KING OF ISRAEL

מֶלֶךְ יִשְׂרָאֵל

Meh-lekh Yees-rah-el

"He saved others," they said, "but He can't save
Himself! He's the King of Israel! Let Him come
down now from the cross, and we will believe in Him."
Matthew 27:42

Dear LORD,

You are an intriguing King, the King of Israel, Meh-lekh
Yees-rah-el. How I pray that Your children of Israel would
see You as King, their King. Thank You for the good plan
that You do have for the salvation of Israel, and please
give me faith to believe that You are working Your perfect will
for the house of Israel even now. I praise Your glorious name.

Glory in His holy name; let the hearts of those who seek
the LORD rejoice. Psalm 105:3

KING OF KINGS

מֶלֶךְ הַמְּלָכִים

Meh-lekh Hahm Lah-kheem

On HIS robe and on HIS thigh HE has this name written:

King of Kings and Lord of Lords.

Revelation 19:16

That You are the King of all the Kings who ever were,

are, or ever will be, is sometimes too much for me

to fully comprehend.

But I am thankful to be Your child.

Thank You for the imperishable inheritance that awaits me

from the Meh-lekh Hahm Lah-kheem, the

King of Kings.

KING OF THE JEWS

מֶלֶךְ הַיְּהוּדִים

Meh-lekh Hy-y'hoo-deem

Above His head they placed the written charge against Him:

THIS IS JESUS, THE KING OF THE JEWS.

Matthew 27:37

God, in Your sovereignty, You chose the Jewish people

from which the lineage of the

Messiah came. You did not choose the Chinese, the African, the Caucasian.

You chose the Jews. my Savior is the Jewish King.

What a wonderful intriguing God You are!

"Father, glorify Your name!" John 12:28

KING OF THE NATIONS

מֶלֶךְ הַגּוֹיִם

Meh-lekh Ha Goy-eem

Who should not revere You,

O King of the nations?

This is Your due.

Among all the wise men of the nations

and in all their kingdoms,

there is no one like You.

Jeremiah 10:7

King of the Nations, Meh-lekh Ha Goy-eem,

How I praise Your name, for there is none like You.

Others may try to usurp Your kingly reign, but they are fools in

Your sight.

Thank You that no matter where I am,

You are King.

LAMB

Seh

And they cried out in a loud voice:

"Salvation belongs to our God, who sits on the throne, and to the Lamb."

Revelation 7:10

Glory to the Lamb who was slain for me, a sinner.

Vicarious atonement—forever atonement. How I praise Your name!

Cry out, "Save us, O God our Savior; gather us and

deliver us from the nations,

that we may give thanks to Your holy name,

that we may glory in Your praise."

1 Chronicles 16:35

LAMB OF GOD

שֶׂה הָאֱלֹהִים

Seh Ha-Eh-lo-heem

The next day John saw Jesus coming toward him and said,
"Look, the Lamb of God, who takes away the sin of the world!"
John 1:29

O LORD, You are the pure, sinless Lamb of God,

Seh Ha-Eh-lo-heem.

You laid down Your life to redeem my life from the curse

of the enemy, once and for all.

How I praise You, Lamb of God!

LAMB WHO WAS SLAIN

Seh Hah-tah-voo-akh

In a loud voice they sang:

"Worthy is the Lamb, who was slain, to receive power and wealth and

wisdom and strength and honor and glory and praise!"

Revelation 5:12

Without Your death, I would not have eternal life. That means everything to me.

How did You do it? How did You lay down Your life?

What a glorious Lamb You are!

LAWGIVER

Hahm-kho-kayk

There is only one Lawgiver and Judge, the one who is able to save and destroy.

James 4:12a

You embody the Torah, the Law. You perfectly fulfill the Law.

Thank You that You perfectly adjudicate the Law.

What a wonderful God we serve!

LIGHT

אוֹר

Or

The light shines in the darkness,
but the darkness has not understood it.

John 1:5

You light up my life because You are the Light.

Even in this world of darkness,

You are still the Light of the world.

LIGHT FOR THE GENTILES

אוֹר גּוֹיִם

Or Goy-eem

"I will also make You a light for the Gentiles,

that You may bring my salvation

to the ends of the earth."

Isaiah 49:6b

Father,

How thankful I am that Your plan of salvation did not

exclude anyone: all peoples are loved by You, and all

peoples are wanted in Your kingdom. To the ends of

the earth You want salvation to go, so You brought Yeshua

Jesus, to be salvation. He is a light to the Jews, He is a

Light for the Gentiles, Or Goy-eem.

What a wonderful God You are.

I will give thanks to the LORD because of His righteousness and

will sing praise to the name of the LORD Most High. Psalm 7:17

LIGHT OF ISRAEL

אוֹר־יִשְׂרָאֵל

Or Yis-rah-el

The Light of Israel will become a fire,

their Holy One a flame.

Isaiah 10:17a

You are the Light of Israel, and the Light of the world.

You set the heavens in orbit.

You chose Jerusalem as Your holy city.

Light of Israel, Or Yis-rah-el, shine forth!

Shine Your light into our darkness,

O Light of Israel!

LIGHT OF THE WORLD

אוֹר הָעוֹלָם

Or Ha~O~lahm

When Yeshua spoke again to the people, He said,

"I am the light of the world.

Whoever follows Me will never walk in darkness, but will have the light of life."

John 8:12

O LORD, there is none like You.

You are the Light of the World.

You are not selective.

You give Your light to all who desire to know You.

Thank You for shining Your light into my world

and into my life.

Thank You, Or Ha~O~lahm, for changing my attitude,

my thoughts, and my life—from darkness to light.

LILY OF THE VALLEYS

שׁוֹשַׁנַּת הָעֲמָקִים

Sho-shah-naht Hah-ah-mah-keem

"I am a rose of Sharon, a lily of the valleys." Song of Solomon 2:1

You are the fairest of all, my Beloved Yeshua. Even though there may be sorrow
in a valley, You are the beautiful lily that grows there.
Let Him kiss me with the kisses of His mouth!

LION OF THE TRIBE OF JUDAH

אַרְיֵה מִשֵׁבֶט יְהוּדָה

Ahr-yay Mee-shay-veht Y'hoo-dah

Then one of the elders said to me,

"Do not weep! See, the Lion of the tribe of Judah, the Root of David,

has triumphed.

He is able to open the scroll and its seven seals."

Revelation 5:5

You are not from the tribe of Aaron or the tribe of Levi.

You are Lion of the tribe of Judah, the majestic King.

How I praise Your name!

We will shout for joy when You are victorious and

will lift up our banners in the name of our God.

May the LORD grant all your requests. Psalm 20:5

LIVING GOD

אֱל-חָי

El Khi

My soul yearns, even faints,

for the courts of the LORD;

my heart and my flesh cry out

for the living God.

Psalm 84:2

O LORD, there are inexpressible yearnings within my heart, and

You know them all.

Only You satisfy, El Khi, Living God.

My soul longs for You, and I desire Your closeness and Your comfort,

O Living God. I love You.

LIVING ONE

הוּא הַחַי

Hoo-Hah-Khi

"I am the Living One; I was dead, and behold I am alive for ever and ever!

And I hold the keys of death and Hades."

Revelation 1:18

Forever You live, forever You reign.

You lived, died, and live again.

I praise You, Living One!

LIVING STONE

Eh-ven Khi-yeem

As you come to Him, the living Stone—rejected by
men but chosen by God and precious to Him—you
also, like living stones, are being built up into a
spiritual house to be a holy priesthood.

1 Peter 2:4-5

A Living Stone, Eh-ven Khi-yeem—this is an oxymoron;
yet in God's kingdom, it all makes sense. You are an Alive Stone,
the Rock, on which all my hope rests. You are my sure foundation;
You are the One upon whom all my cares reside, whom all my faith
looks up to. How I praise You for allowing me the privilege of
being in Your family of living stones!

I will declare Your name to my brothers; in the congregation
I will praise You. Psalm 22:22

LORD

YHVH A-do-ni

"I appeared to Abraham, to Isaac and to Jacob as God Almighty,
but by My name the LORD I did not make Myself known to them."
Exodus 6:3

For all of my loved ones who don't know You personally,
will You reveal Yourself to them?
O LORD, YHVH, A-do-ni, please reveal who You are to them,
for knowing You is the greatest joy of my life.
I trust You.

LORD GOD

יְהוָה אֱלֹהִים

A-do-ni Eh-lo-heem

When the LORD God made the earth and the heavens—

and no shrub of the field had yet appeared on the earth

and no plant of the field had yet sprung up,

for the LORD God had not sent rain on the earth

and there was no man to work the ground,

but streams came up from the earth and watered the whole surface of the ground—

the LORD God formed the man from the dust of the ground and breathed into his

nostrils the breath of life, and the man became a living being.

Genesis 2:4b-7

Just as You made the earth and the heavens,

LORD God, You made me, too. You formed me from the womb;

Your hands made me.

A-do-ni Eh-lo-heem, I praise Your wonderful name and

Your marvelous works. And You even know what awaits me today.

Thank You that I can rest in calm assurance and trust You.

Therefore I will praise You among the nations, O LORD;

I will sing praises to Your name. Psalm 18:49

LORD GOD ALMIGHTY

יְי אֱלֹהִים צְבָאוֹת

Ah-do-ni Eh-lo-heem Ts-vah-ote

Restore us, O LORD God Almighty; make Your face shine upon us,

that we may be saved.

Psalm 80:19

You are the Almighty God, the God of Hosts, the God of armies.

Thank You that You never leave me defenseless in my time of trial.

I love You and could never repay You for Your being my defense in time of war.

LORD GOD OF ABRAHAM, ISAAC AND ISRAEL

יְהוָה אֱלֹהֵי
אַבְרָהָם יִצְחָק
וְיִשְׂרָאֵל

A-do-ni Eh-lo-hay Ahv-rah-hahm
Yeets-khahk V-Yees-rah-el

At the time of sacrifice,

the prophet Elijah stepped forward and prayed:

"O LORD, God of Abraham, Isaac and Israel,

let it be known today that You are God in Israel

and that I am Your servant

and have done all these things at Your command."

1 Kings 18:36

What a wonder You are, LORD God of Abraham, Isaac and Israel,

A-do-ni Eh-lo-hay Ahv-rah-hahm Yeets-khahk V-Yees-rah-el.

From the patriarchs to today, You are the same LORD.

How marvelous is Your name!

LORD GOD OF gods

יְהוָה אֵל אֱלֹהִים

A-do-ni El Eh-lo-heem

"The LORD God of gods, the LORD God of gods,
He knows, and let Israel itself know—
if it is in rebellion, or if in treachery against the LORD,
do not save us this day."
Joshua 22:22 NKJV

When I stop to think of all the concerns of others,
the major needs and events in the world, how comforted
I am to know that You care.
Just as You know every sparrow,
You know the hairs on my head.
Thank You, A-do-ni El Eh-lo-heem, for
Your sovereign love and care for me.
How I praise Your name!

LORD GOD OF HEAVEN

יְהוָה אֱלֹהֵי הַשָּׁמַיִם

A-do-ni El-lo-hay HaShah-mi-eem

"The LORD, the God of heaven,

who brought me out of my father's household and my native land

and who spoke to me and promised me on oath, saying,

'To Your offspring I will give this land'—

He will send His angel before you..."

Genesis 24:7

You are LORD over all the earth and heavens.

All I need to do is look up and realize that

You are.

You, A-do-ni Eh-lo-hay HaShah-mi-eem, see everything.

As You spoke to Abraham,

You still speak today.

How I praise You for Your wonderful ways.

He provided redemption for His people;

He ordained His covenant forever—holy and awesome is His name.

Psalm 111:9

LORD GOD OF ISRAEL

יְהוָה אֱלֹהֵי יִשְׂרָאֵל

A-do-ni Eh-lo-hay Yis-rah-el

Joshua said to all the people,

"This is what the LORD, the God of Israel, says:

'Long ago your forefathers, including Terah the

father of Abraham and Nahor,

lived beyond the River and worshiped other gods.' "

Joshua 24:2

LORD, in these times when other activities and temptations

try to steal my love away from You,

help me to cling even closer to You.

I choose to serve A-do-ni Eh-lo-hay Yis-rah-el,

the LORD, the God of Israel.

I desire You, O LORD, for only You

satisfy the longing in my soul.

Thank You for the peace that You always give.

LORD GOD OF OUR FATHERS

יְהוָה אֱלֹהֵי אֲבֹתֵינוּ

A-do-ni Eh-lo-hay Ah-vo-tay-noo

Praise be to the LORD, the God of our fathers,

who has put it into the king's heart to bring honor

to the house of the LORD in Jerusalem in this way.

Ezra 7:27

From generation to generation, You reign supreme over all the earth.

What a comfort it is to know that You are the same God,

A-do-ni Eh-lo-hay Ah-vo-tay-noo.

From Abraham to Moses to David,

the patriarchs and I have the same LORD.

How blessed I am.

"Praise be to the name of God for ever and ever;

wisdom and power are His." Daniel 2:20

LORD GOD OF RETRIBUTION

אֵל גְּמֻלוֹת יְהוָה

El G'moo-lote Ah-do-ni

"For the LORD is a God of retribution;

He will repay in full."

Jeremiah 51:56b

Thank You for showing me that revenge is not my prerogative.
You are the LORD God of Retribution, El G'moo-lote
Ah-do-ni; I do not need to concern myself with my enemies.

You command me to pray for my enemies, but to not seek
revenge. Thank You that You know how to repay my enemies.
And my chief desire is that they would know Your love, for
You are the One who can change hearts. And that is an
inside job that takes the Master Surgeon's work, not a job
for someone like me.
So do Your work on my enemies, O LORD God of Retribution.
Change their heart of stone to a heart of flesh, and give them love for You.
I love Your wonderful name.

LORD GOD OF TRUTH

יְהֹוָה--אֵל אֱמֶת

A-do-ni Ayl Eh-meht

Into Your hands I commit my spirit;

redeem me, O LORD, the God of truth.

Psalm 31:5

How glorious it is to know You,

LORD God of truth, A-do-ni Ayl Eh-meht.

my heart cries out for truth; then

I run to Your arms, and

I find everything I need:

every comfort,

every good word.

Thank You.

LORD GOD OF Your FATHERS

יְהוָה אֱלֹהֵי-אֲבֹתֶיךָ

A-do-ni Eh-lo-hay Ah-vo-teh-khah

Write on them all the words of this law
when you have crossed over to enter
the land the LORD your God is giving you,
a land flowing with milk and honey,
just as the LORD, the God of your fathers, promised you.

Deuteronomy 27:3

You are the wonderful God,
the LORD, the God of Your Fathers,
A-do-ni Eh-lo-hay Ah-vo-teh-khah.
It is a comfort to know that You have been in the past,
You are in the present
and You will be in the future.

LORD IS MY BANNER

A-do-ni Nee-see

Moses built an altar and called it

The LORD is my Banner.

Exodus 17:15

Father, thank You that in this imperfect world,

You are my Banner, my Standard.

Your perfection is my goal, and I thank You,

A-do-ni Nee-see.

I have You to look up to—through it all. Thank You.

LORD IS ONE

יְהוָה אֶחָד וּשְׁמוֹ אֶחָד

A-do-ni Eh-khad Oo-sh'mo Eh-khad

And the LORD shall be King over all the earth.
In that day it shall be--
"The LORD is one," And His name one.
Zechariah 14:9 NKJV

What a marvelous mystery! God my Father; God as Yeshua
who came to show me how to live; God as the Spirit,
Ruakh HaKodesh, who empowers me to live the godly life.
Three in One: what a marvelous mystery!
A-do-ni Eh-khad Oo-sh'mo Eh-khad, the LORD is One,
His name One.
Thank You, LORD, that I don't have to understand this with my head
to know it in my heart. How marvelous is Your name!

Your name, O LORD, endures forever,
Your renown, O LORD, through all generations.
Psalm 135:13

LORD IS PEACE

יְהוָה שָׁלוֹם

Ah-do-ni Shalom

So Gideon built an altar to the LORD there and called it

The LORD is peace.

Judges 6:24a

Ah-do-ni Shalom, the LORD is Peace. When my soul is in turmoil,

when distress torments my soul—how thankful I am to know that

You have everything under control.

In the midst of my storms, help me to be like Peter, to keep my eyes on You.

For You will not always take the storm away,

but You always give me the power to walk through the storm.

And You give me the power to walk on the waters through the

storm—but only if I keep my eyes on You.

Thank You for the peace that You give,

for the LORD is Peace, Ah-do-ni Shalom.

For the sake of Your name, O LORD, forgive my iniquity,

though it is great. Psalm 25:11

LORD IS THERE

A-do-ni Shah-mah

"The distance all around will be 18,000 cubits.

"And the name of the city from that time on will be:

THE LORD IS THERE."

Ezekiel 48:35

A-do-ni Shah-mah, the LORD Is There—what a comfort

to know that deep in my soul, whatever trouble assails me,

You are there with me.

Just as You chose Jerusalem to be the city in which You dwelt,

You also dwell in the heart of every child of God.

How I praise You for Your eternal truths.

Even when I doubt Your presence,

I trust Your heart.

I know that if I am patient, I will always see Your presence.

May I never ever doubt that You are always there for me.

LORD MY GOD

יְהוָה אֱלֹהַי

A-do-ni Eh-lo-hi

Then the LORD my God will come, and all the holy ones with Him.

Zechariah 14:5c

To know You personally, and to see You in everything,

makes life the greatest adventure ever.

What a blessing it is to know You, and to know that

You know me, and love me, just the way I am.

A-do-ni Eh-lo-hi, thank You for loving me.

I will praise God's name in song and glorify Him with thanksgiving.

Psalm 69:30

LORD MY ROCK

יְהוָה צוּרִי

A-do-ní Tsu-ree

Praise be to the LORD my Rock,

who trains my hands for war,

my fingers for battle.

Psalm 144:1

How blessed I am to know that You are

my Rock and my fortress.

You are the one who equips me to do Your work.

Thank You that You equip the called, not call the equipped.

Today, help me to realize that You have provided for my every need,

one step at a time.

A-do-ní Tsu-ree, how I thank You!

LORD OF ALL

אֲדוֹן כֹּל

Ah-don Kohl

You know the message God sent to the people of
Israel, telling the good news of peace through
Yeshua HaMashiach Jesus Christ, who is Lord of all.

Acts 10:36

You are Lord of All, not just Lord of this race, or Lord of
that language or nation, but You are Lord of All, Ah-don Kohl.
How grateful I am that You don't choose through selective
service, but that You desire all to come to know You.
How I love Your name.

LORD OF HEAVEN

מָרֵא-שְׁמַיָּא

Mah-ray Sh'My-yah

"You have set yourself up against the Lord of heaven."

Daniel 5:23a

You, Lord of Heaven, Mah-ray Sh'My-yah, hold my life in Your hand.

As You reign on earth and in heaven, help me to desire Your ways only.

Help me to surrender my will to Your divine will.

Make my "want to" to line up with Your will.

How I love Your name, O Lord of Heaven.

Help us, O God our Savior, for the glory of Your name;

deliver us and forgive our sins for Your name's sake.

Psalm 79:9

LORD OF HOSTS

יְהֹוָה צְבָאֹת

A-do-ni Ts-vah-ote

And one cried to another and said:

"Holy, holy, holy is the LORD of hosts;

The whole earth is full of His glory!"

Isaiah 6:3 NKJV

A-do-ni Ts-vah-ote, LORD of Hosts,

how glorious it is to be in Your presence.

My heart and my flesh sing for joy to You,

for there is none like You.

You, LORD of Hosts,

LORD of all heavenly armies and heavenly hosts–

You do battle for me.

As the serapHim cry: M'lo khawl ha-oretz b'vodo–

The whole earth is full of Your glory!

I shall never let the rocks out-praise me.

How I love You, O LORD of Hosts!

LORD OF KINGS

מָרֵא מַלְכִין

Mah-ray Mahl-kheen

The king said to Daniel,

"Surely Your God is the God of gods

and the LORD of kings and a revealer of mysteries."

Daniel 2:47a

Dear LORD, You rule over all sovereigns, kings, princes,

rulers on earth and in heaven. Thank You that it is You that I serve; may I always be a

faithful follower, an eager

servant, to be pleasing to You. How I praise Your name.

LORD OF LORDS

אֲדֹנֵי הָאֲדֹנִים

A-don Ha-ah-do-neem

On His robe and on His thigh He has this name written:

King of Kings and LORD of LORDS.

Revelation 19:16

You are the LORD.

You are my master.

You know me personally.

There is no other need that must be fulfilled,

for You satisfy my every need.

A-don Ha-ah-do-neem, LORD of Lords,

Thank You for being LORD to me.

I love You.

"I am the LORD; that is My name!

I will not give My glory to another or My praise to idols."

Isaiah 42:8

LORD OF THE WHOLE WORLD

אֲדוֹן כָּל- הָאָרֶץ

Ah-don kole Ha'ah-retz

"These are the four spirits of heaven, going out from standing in the
presence of the Lord of the whole world."
Zechariah 6:5

What a privilege it is to know You,
Ah-don kole Ha'ah-retz, the Lord of the Whole World.
You are in control of any and everything that should come against me.
Why should I fear any longer? Your hand controls nature,
Your sovereign protection is always there.
I praise Your wonderful name.

I write these things to you who believe in the name of the Son of God
so that you may know that you have eternal life. 1 John 5:13

LORD OUR GOD

יְהוָה אֱלֹהֵינוּ

A-do-ni Eh-lo-hay-noo

Exalt the LORD our God
and worship at His footstool;
He is holy.
Psalm 99:5

LORD God, how I praise You for this wonderful
plan of redemption that You had before time began.
Thank You that You made a way where there seemed to be no way.
A-do-ni Eh-lo-hay-noo, LORD Our God,
You did it back then, and I thank You that
You continue to work like that today.
It is a privilege to be Your child.

LORD OUR MAKER

יְהֹוָה עֹשֵׂנוּ

A-do-ni O-say-noo

Come, let us bow down in worship,

let us kneel before the LORD our Maker.

Psalm 95:6

How comforting it is know that You are my Maker.

You know me better than I know myself.

Your desires for me are higher than my desires for me.

A-do-ni O-say-noo, help me to live this day in submission

to Your will, for You made me.

You lead me in paths of righteousness,

for Your name's sake.

Thank You for loving me.

Do not profane My holy name.

Leviticus 22:32a

LORD OUR RIGHTEOUSNESS

יְהוָה צִדְקֵנוּ

A-do-ni Tseed-kay-noo

In His days Judah will be saved

and Israel will live in safety.

This is the name by which He will be called:

The LORD Our Righteousness.

Jeremiah 23:6

A-do-ni Tseed-kay-noo, the LORD Our Righteousness.

May I always remember it is never me but always Thee.

In my goodness, it is Thee.

How I praise You that I have no goodness apart from You.

How I praise You that Your righteousness can be mine!

Help me to be obedient to You,

in thought, word and deed.

LORD WHO HEALS You

יְהוָה רֹפְאֶךָ

A-do-ni Rof-eh-khah

He said,

"If you listen carefully to the voice of the LORD your God

and do what is right in His eyes,

if you pay attention to His commands and keep all His decrees,

I will not bring on you any of the diseases I brought on the Egyptians,

for I am the LORD, who heals you."

Exodus 15:26

Thank You, LORD, that when I have nowhere else to turn for help

for the sinful things that still combat my soul,

You are there.

Father, temptations assail me daily, yet

You are the LORD Who Heals Me.

A-do-ni Rof-eh-khah, help me, heal me from the things of the past and

from things hidden now.

Thank You that You do heal.

LORD WHO MAKES YOU HOLY

יְהוָה מְקַדִּשְׁכֶם

A-do-ni M'kah-deesh-khehm

Do not profane My holy name.

I must be acknowledged as holy by the Israelites.

I am the LORD, who makes you holy.

Leviticus 22:32

It is not my acts of charity that make me holy.

It is the blood of the Lamb, Yeshua, that sanctifies me.

Thank You, LORD Who Makes Me Holy,

A-do-ni M'kah-deesh-khehm.

What a marvelous wonder You are to me!

Free from the guilty stain of sin, free to walk in newness of life!

Thank You for helping me to live a life set apart to You.

Those who know Your name will trust in You,

for You, LORD, have never forsaken those who seek You.

Psalm 9:10

LORD WILL PROVIDE

A-do-ni Yee-rah-eh

So Abraham called that place

The LORD Will Provide. And to this day it is said,

"On the mountain of the LORD it will be provided."

Genesis 22:14

On the mount, You were seen! LORD, how grateful I am for

Your hand of provision. Sometimes we cannot actually see You, but we see how

You provide. We see You!

You give and You withhold—all for my best.

You call me to obey, not to sacrifice. A-do-ni Yee-rah-eh.

How I praise You for providing beyond what I could hope for, dream of or ask.

Sometimes I feel like I am being backed into a corner, with nowhere to go.

And that is exactly the time that You always come through for me.

How wonderful it is to know You.

Praise be to His glorious name forever;

may the whole earth be filled with His glory.

Amen and Amen.

Psalm 72:19

LORD YOUR GOD

יְהוָה אֱלֹהֶיךָ

A-do-ni Eh-lo-heh-kha

"I am the LORD your God,
who brought you out of egypt,
out of the land of slavery."

Exodus 20:2

How glorious is Your hand of deliverance.

I have much inner assurance just knowing that

You see me.

You know me, and You will perfect that which concerns me.

A-do-ni Eh-lo-heh-kha,

the LORD Your God,

Thank You for being sovereign over all of

Your children.

LORD YOUR MAKER

יְהוָה עֹשֶׂךָ

Ah-do-ni Oh-seh-kha

"I, even I, am He who comforts you. who are you
that you fear mortal men, the sons of men, who are
but grass, that you forget the LORD your Maker?"

Isaiah 51:12-13a

Forgive me for not deeming
You worthy of the respect that
You deserve. You fight for me;
You give me favor; You do all things for me.
How blessed I am, Ah-do-ni Oh-seh-kha,
LORD Your Maker. How wonderful is Your name!

LORD YOUR REDEEMER

גֹּאֲלֵךְ יְהוָה

Go-ah-laykh Ah-do-ni

"I will have compassion on You,"
says the LORD Your redeemer.
Isaiah 54:8b

You bestow the ultimate compassion upon me, LORD, by allowing me to live the exchanged life with Yeshua. All that I deserved, He got, and all that He deserved, I got: redemption, life eternal. How can I ever thank You, Go-ah-laykh Ah-do-ni, LORD Your Redeemer?

All the nations You have made will come and worship
before You, O LORD; they will bring glory to Your name. Psalm 86:9

MAGNIFICENT IN WISDOM

הִגְדִּיל תּוּשִׁיָּה

Heeg-deel Too-shee-yah

All this also comes from the LORD Almighty,

wonderful in counsel and magnificent in wisdom.

Isaiah 28:29

For every challenge that I have, You are the answer. You give the answer.

Your wisdom is higher than any other's on earth. How Magnificent in

Wisdom are You, Heeg-deel Too-shee-yah. Thank You that You make

me wiser than my enemies. You give me daily wisdom, too.

How I praise Your name!

Ascribe to the Lord the glory due His name;

worship the LORD in the splendor of His holiness. Psalm 29:2

MAJESTIC

Ah-deer

O LORD, our Lord,

how majestic is Your name in all the earth!

Psalm 8:1

When we pray in the name of Yeshua, there is

power in His name.

The same power that set His glory, His Kavod,

in the heavens, is the same power available to me.

How Majestic, Ah-deer, is Your name!

I thank You that I know You by name.

Give thanks to the LORD, call on His name;

make known among the nations what He has done.

Psalm 105:1

MAKER OF ALL THINGS

יוֹצֵר הַכֹּל

Yo-tsayr Ha-kol

He who is the Portion of Jacob is not like these,

for He is the Maker of all things.

Jeremiah 10:16a

You, the Maker of All Things, Yo-tsayr Ha-kol,

You made me.

Your hands fashioned me. You formed me in my mother's womb.

Since You created me, why should I not trust You

with everything in my life?

Thank You for giving me Shalom, peace, in the midst

of all that goes on within me.

I surrender my life into Your hands,

Maker of All Things.

MAN OF SORROWS

אִישׁ מַכְאֹבוֹת

Eesh Mahk-oh-vote

He was despised and rejected by men,
a man of sorrows, and familiar with suffering.
Like one from whom men hide their faces He was despised,
and we esteemed Him not.

Isaiah 53:3

If I had seen You back then, I would not have esteemed You,
I would have paid You no attention. Forgive me!
It is never about me, but only about You! Your Love!
You laid down Your life for me; I owe You my life in return.
How I love You, dear Man of Sorrows.

MEDIATOR

מֵלִיץ

May-leetz

For there is one God and one mediator between
God and men, the man
Yeshua HaMashiach, Jesus Christ.
1 Timothy 2:5

Only You see the errors of my ways, my sins. And You
who see everything, intercede on My behalf to God the
Father. What a wonder You are! You are My Mediator,
May-leetz. Thank You for being the go-between, being my
Mediator, pleading my case to the Father. Thank You that
Your blood paid the debt I could not pay, to live the life
that I always wanted to live. I love You, LORD.

I will praise You, O Lord My God, with all my heart;
I will glorify Your name forever. Psalm 86:12

MERCIFUL

Rahk-mahn

For this reason He had to be made like His brothers
in every way, in order that He might become a merciful
and faithful high priest in service to God, and that
He might make atonement for the sins of the people.
Hebrews 2:17

How wonderful is Your name, O Most Merciful God. You
are abundant in mercy, You are full of mercy. What I mostly
deserve is punishment, but You put Your arms around me, and
love me, and give me unconditional acceptance, not because
of what I have done, but all because of the Blood of Yeshua.
Thank You that entry to heaven is not dependent on my work,
but all because of the love that was poured out at Calvary.
You are Merciful, Rahk-mahn, and I praise Your name!

"And whoever welcomes a little child like this in My name
welcomes Me." Matthew 18:5

MIGHTY GOD

El Guee-bor

For to us a child is born,

to us a son is given,

and the government will be on His shoulders.

And He will be called Wonderful Counselor,

Mighty God.

Isaiah 9:6a

You are the Mighty One, the Champion, El Guee-bor,

the Valiant One.

How I praise You that when I am weak, then You are strong.

There is nothing else that I need other than the knowledge

that You know me and You love me.

What confidence You give to me.

Thank You for the assurance that You go before me in all I do.

Thank You, Mighty God.

O great and powerful God, whose name is the LORD Almighty,

great are Your purposes and mighty are Your deeds. Jeremiah 32:18b-19a

MIGHTY ONE OF ISRAEL

אֲבִיר יִשְׂרָאֵל

Ah-veer Yis-rah-el

Therefore, the Lord, the LORD Almighty,
the Mighty One of Israel, declares:
"Ah, I will get relief from My foes
and avenge Myself on My enemies."
Isaiah 1:24

Sometimes I am stunned to think that You have
enemies, but Your word says You do. I am glad that
You are the Mighty One of Israel, Ah-veer Yis-rah-el,
and You are the Mighty One of everyone else who
loves You, too. What a wonderful God You are.

MIGHTY ONE OF JACOB

אֲבִיר יַעֲקֹב

Ah-veer Yah-ah-cove

"I will make your oppressors eat their own flesh;
they will be drunk on their own blood, as with wine.
Then all mankind will know that I, the LORD, am your Savior,
your redeemer, the Mighty One of Jacob."

Isaiah 49:26

O LORD, what promises You give us!
You promise to destroy our enemies.
Thank You for these promises.
I can trust You, O Mighty One of Jacob!

MINISTER OF THE SANCTUARY

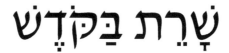

Shah-rayt Bah-ko-desh

We have such a High Priest,

who is seated at the right hand of the throne of the Majesty in the heavens,

a Minister of the sanctuary

and of the true tabernacle which the Lord erected, and not man.

Hebrews 8:1-2 NKJV

What a blessing it is to know You, our great High Priest.

You are the Minister of the Sanctuary,

Shah-rayt Bah-ko-desh.

I thank You that You do for me what I cannot do for myself.

You minister before God and help me.

Thank You that You are seated in heavenly places.

What a wonder You are.

MORNING STAR

אוֹר נֹגַהּ וְכוֹכַב הַשָׁחַר

Or No-gah v'kho-chahv Hah-shah-khar

"I, Yeshua, have sent My angel to give you this testimony for the churches.

I am the Root and the Offspring of David,

and the bright Morning Star."

Revelation 22:16

You light up my life. You are the first light of the morning,

the bright Morning Star. Without You, I have no light.

I worship You!

MOST HIGH

El-yone

I will be glad and rejoice in You;
I will sing praise to Your name, O Most High.
Psalm 9:2

O Most High, El-yone, You are omnipotent!
You are all-powerful.
You are higher than all others in heaven and on earth.
Thank You, LORD, for going to battle for me.
You turn back my enemies!
I shall not trust in my abilities, but
I choose to put my trust in You, O Most High!

MY BELOVED

דּוֹדִי

Doh-dee

Now let me sing to my Well-beloved
A song of my Beloved regarding His vineyard.
Isaiah 5:1a

There is no one closer to me than You.
And besides You, my Beloved, Doh-dee,
I desire no one else.
You are my Beloved, and I desire to be
true to You all of my life.
And what is more, You look upon me and call me
Beloved.
Thank You for Your boundless, infinite love.

"Our Father in heaven,
hallowed be Your name." Matthew 6:9

MY CHOSEN ONE

B'khee-ree

"Here is My servant, whom I uphold,
My chosen one in whom I delight."
Isaiah 42:1

What a wonderful God You are. Those in
Your kingdom are the ones You have chosen.
We love because
You first loved us.

MY DELIVERER

M'fahl-tee

The LORD is my rock, my fortress and
my deliverer.
Psalm 18:2a

How often You amaze me! When I think that there
is no hope for me, You always come through for me,
and You deliver me from evil, from danger—from
myself!
You are my Deliverer, M'fahl-tee. You are the One
who safely carries me to the safe place, to Your refuge.
Words cannot express, at times, just how much
I love You, and yet You love me even more.
How I praise Your name.

Let them praise the name of the LORD,
for His name alone is exalted. Psalm 148:13

MY FATHER'S GOD

Eh-lo-hay Ah-vee

He is my God, and I will praise Him,

my father's God, and I will exalt Him.

Exodus 15:2b

From eternity past to eternity future, You are God.

You know everything. You were

my Father's God, Eh-lo-hay Ah-vee, and

You are my God. I praise Your name.

MY FORTRESS

מְצוּדָתִי

M'tsoo-dah-tee

The LORD is my rock, my fortress and my
deliverer; my God is my rock,
in whom I take refuge.

Psalm 18:2a

You are my Fortress, M'tsoo-dah-tee. There
are so many times that I am up against unseen
forces, and yet I know that You are really there,
protecting me. Thank You that You have given
me the understanding that it is You who protects
me, and not the other way around. I love You.

Give me an undivided heart that I may fear Your name. Psalm 86:11b

MY GOD

אֱלֹהַי

Eh-lo-hi

With Your help I can advance against

a troop;

with my God I can scale a wall.

2 Samuel 22:30

How blessed I am to have You as my God,

Eh-lo-hi. No matter what assails me, no

matter what challenges me, taunts me, attacks

me—You are my God, and I know You will

guide me until death. How blessed I am to know

You personally.

Save us, O LORD our God, and gather us from the nations, that we may

give thanks to Your holy name and glory in Your praise. Psalm 106:47

MY GOD OF MERCY

אֱלֹהֵי חַסְדִּי

Eh-lo-hay Khahs-dee

My God of mercy shall come to meet me;
God shall let me see my desire on my enemies.
Psalm 59:10

Thank You that You are my God of Mercy.
Eh-lo-hay Khahs-dee.
You surround me with lovingkindness all the days of my life.
Thank You for the mercy that You give to Your children.
How measureless is Your love.
Help me today to be a vessel of Your love and mercy,
in gratitude for all that You have done for me.

You shall not misuse the name of the LORD your God,
for the LORD will not hold anyone guiltless who misuses His name.
Deuteronomy 5:11

MY JOY AND MY DELIGHT

שִׂמְחַת גִּילִי

Seem-khaht Guee-lee

Then will I go to the altar of God,

to God, my joy and my delight.

Psalm 43:4a

You are my Joy and my Delight.

There is no one I desire but You.

You bring joy and glee to me like no one else.

A bad day with You is better than a good day without You.

You are the Best!

MY LOVING GOD

אֱלֹהֵי חַסְדִּי

Eh-lo-hay Khahs-dee

O my Strength, I sing praise to You;
You, O God, are my fortress, my loving God.
Psalm 59:17

When I am afraid, when I doubt–
help me to know that You are the God Who Loves Me,
Eh-lo-hay Khahs-dee. Your ways are perfect,
and even if I don't sense Your nearness, call to
my remembrance Your former loving ways to me.
How do You love me?
You gave Your Son Yeshua for me.
How I love Your name!

MY ROCK

צוּרִי

Tsoo-ree

The Lord lives! Praise be to my Rock!

Exalted be God my Savior!

Psalm 18:46

You are the foundation of everything in my life.

From You I have strength to do everything that You call me to do.

Without You, without Your strong foundation,

I am on shaky ground. How I praise You, Tsoo-ree, my Rock!

MY SALVATION

לִי לִישׁוּעָה

Lee Lee-shoo-ah

The LORD is my strength and my song;
He has become my salvation.
Exodus 15:2a

Just as the children of Israel sang this after seeing
Your act of deliverance and help for them at the
Red Sea, LORD, this is my song, too. You are
My Salvation, Lee Lee-shoo-ah.
You save me from death, from my self, from my
enemies, from hidden danger. How I praise Your
wonderful saving name!

No one is like You, O LORD; You are great, and
Your name is mighty in power. Jeremiah 10:6

MY SAVIOR

Yeesh-ee

And Miriam (Mary) said,
"My soul glorifies the Lord
and my spirit rejoices in God my Savior."
Luke 1:46-47

Sometimes I can't even fathom how much You really
have done for me, my Savior, Yeesh-ee. How I praise
You for taking my life out of the pit that the enemy had
lured me into. How I praise You for the abundant life
that You now allow me to live. And all this is because of
Thee, not me. What a wonderful Savior You are!

MY SERVANT

עַבְדִּי

Ahv-dee

"Here is my servant whom I have chosen,

the one I love, in whom I delight."

Matthew 12:18a

Yeshua, You are the perfect Servant of God.

Help me to follow in Your footsteps.

May my life be poured out in service to others.

MY SHIELD

מָגִנִּי

Mah-guee-nee

He is my shield and the horn of my salvation,
my stronghold.
Psalm 18:2b

How thankful I am that You are my Shield. You protect me
against my enemies—against their hurtful words, taunts,
accusations and attacks. my Shield, Mah-guee-nee—
how thankful I am that You are in control of every activity
of my life. Help me to walk in victory today.

"Then I will purify the lips of the peoples, that all of
them may call on the name of the LORD." Zephaniah 3:9a

MY STRENGTH

Ah-zee

The LORD is my strength.

Exodus 15:2a

I have no strength of my own. But when I tap into You,

my Strength, Ah-zee, I can do all things through Messiah

who strengthens me.

Keep me always attached to the power source, LORD.

MY STRONGHOLD

Mees-gah-bee

He is my shield and the horn of my salvation,

my stronghold.

Psalm 18:2b

When I am afraid, I will put my trust in You.

You are the One who holds on to me.

So I run to You in troubled times,

for You are my Stronghold.

MY WELL-BELOVED

Y-Dee-dee

Now let me sing to my Well-beloved

A song of My Beloved regarding His vineyard:

my Well-beloved has a vineyard

On a very fruitful hill.

Isaiah 5:1 NKJV

There is none like You.

No one treats me the way You do.

You are my Well-Beloved, Lee-dee-dee.

How can I express my love to You?

Thank You for Your steadfast lovingkindness.

I long to be in Your presence.

Thank You for the bounty that is found only in You.

NAZARENE

נָצְרִי

Nots-ree

And He went and lived in a town called Nazareth. So was
fulfilled what was said through the prophets:
"He will be called a Nazarene."
Matthew 2:23

To know You as Nazarene, Nots-ree, tells me where You
lived, not Your denomination, for in You we are all One—
Eh-khad. I am thankful that Your beginnings were not in a
kingly palace, but in a humble town where You worked as a
laborer, a carpenter. What a blessing to know Your name.

NO OTHER NAME

לֹא שֵׁם אַחֵר

Lo Shame akayr

"Salvation is found in no one else, for there is

no other name under heaven given to men

by which we must be saved."

Acts 4:12

What a wonderful blessing it is to know Your name, the
name by which I must be saved, the name of Yeshua, Jesus.
There is no lovelier name, No Other Name, Lo Shame akayr,
no higher name than Yours.
What a comfort it is to me, when I am in the midst of turmoil,
and I say Your name over and over again. Thank You for the
wonderful peace that Your name gives me.

"The LORD gave and the LORD has taken away;
may the name of the LORD be praised." Job 1:21b

NUMBERED WITH THE TRANSGRESSORS

אֶת-פֹּשְׁעִים נִמְנָה

Eht Posh-eem Neem-nah

He poured out His soul unto death,

And He was numbered with the transgressors.

Isaiah 53:12b NKJV

Innocent, yet Numbered with the Transgressors,

Eht Posh-eem Neem-nah.

The Lamb of God, guilty of nothing.

All You did was love.

All You do is love.

All You will ever do is love.

Worthy is the Lamb of God.

O LORD, THE GOD OF TRUTH

יְהוָה--אֵל אֱמֶת

Ah-do-ni El Eh-meht

Free me from the trap that is set for me,

for You are my refuge.

Into Your hands I commit my spirit;

Redeem me, O LORD, the God of truth.

Psalm 31:4-5

Whom have I in heaven but You? There are so many
snares around me, how can I know who to trust?
How wonderful it is to know You, O LORD, the God
of Truth, Ah-do-ni El Eh-meht. If I can be patient
enough to wait for Your will, I know that it will be
the perfect place for me. May my will be neutral,
until You bring forth the answer to these needs.

I wait on Your good name.

O WATCHER OF MEN

נֹצֵר הָאָדָם

No-tzair Hah-ah-dahm

"If I have sinned, what have I done to You, O watcher of men?"

Job 7:20a

Nothing that I do escapes Your view. Your eyes behold everyone.

I am comforted by this, though. I am never alone.

My human mind cannot comprehend this.

You are awesome, God!

"You shall not misuse the name of the LORD Your God,

for the LORD will not hold anyone guiltless

who misuses His name." Deuteronomy 5:11

ONE

אֶחָד

Eh-khahd

And the LORD shall be King over all the earth.

In that day it shall be--

"The LORD is one,"

And His name one.

Zechariah 14:9 NKJV

Hear, O Israel: the LORD, our God, is One.

He is Eh-khahd: how glorious is that word,

Eh-khahd.

United...Only....Altogether....One.

You are Eh-khahd, a United One.

There is no one like You.

How I praise Your name.

ONLY BEGOTTEN SON

בֵּן יָחִיד לְאָבִיו

Ben Yah-kheed L'Ah-veev

And the Word was made flesh, and dwelt among
us, and we beheld His glory, the glory as of the only
begotten of the Father, full of grace and truth.
John 1:14 KJV

That God can even have a Son astounds me, yet I
thank You for the grace that enables me to understand
this concept by faith. And that You, Yeshua, are the
Only Begotten Son, Ben Yah-kheed L'Ah-veev, is sometimes
too awesome to comprehend. Thank You for showing
me the way to the Father. How I praise Your name!

"I am a great king, says the LORD almighty, and
My name is to be feared among the nations." Malachi 1:14

ONLY GOD OUR SAVIOR

אֱלֹהִים
לְבַדּוֹ הַגֹּאֵל
אֹתָנוּ

Eh-lo-heem L-vah-doe Ha-go-ail O-tah-noo

To the only God our Savior

be glory, majesty, power and authority,

through Jesus Christ our Lord,

before all ages, now and forevermore!

Amen.

Jude 1:25

You are the Only God, One God, yet You choose to call

Yourself Eh-lo-heem, multiple El, multiple God.

You are Our Savior; we love You.

ONLY WISE GOD

אֱלֹהִים אֶחָד וְהֶחָכָם

Eh-lo-heem Eh-khahd V'Heh-Khah-Khahm

Now unto the King eternal, immortal, invisible,

the only wise God,

be honour and glory for ever and ever. Amen.

1 Timothy 1:17

Thank You, dear God, that as long as I seek You,

You give me help beyond my wildest dreams.

Thank You that when I ask for wisdom,

You give it.

Eh-lo-heem Eh-khahd V'heh-Khah-Khahm,

the Only Wise God,

thank You for Your help in all of my human circumstances.

You are the plus to all the minuses in my life.

How I thank You for Your wisdom:

past, present, future.

But You, O Sovereign LORD,

deal well with me for Your name's sake;

out of the goodness of Your love, deliver me.

Psalm 109:21

OPPRESSED

Nee-gahs

He was oppressed and afflicted,

yet He did not open His mouth.

Isaiah 53:7a

You were oppressed, Nee-gahs.

Death was imminent.

You opened not Your mouth.

What an example that You have given me.

When people come against me, Your example has

demonstrated humility.

May I be like You when attacked.

OUR DWELLING PLACE

Mah-on

LORD, You have been our dwelling place
throughout all generations.

Psalm 90:1

The same God who was the Dwelling Place for Moses
is the same God to me.
When I am oppressed, when I am afraid, and when
I don't know what to do, it is a comfort to run to You,
Mah-on, Dwelling Place, and rest there.
Thank You that there is safety in the cleft of Your rock.

OUR FATHER

Ah-vee-noo

But You are our Father,

though Abraham does not know us or Israel acknowledge us;

You, O LORD, are our Father.

Isaiah 63:16a

Ah-vee-noo, Our Father: how precious it is to know

You in this way. You created me, You know me from

the womb, You have known me longer than anyone

else on the earth. I thank You for the lessons You

allow me to learn; sometimes Your chastening is

not pleasant or easy, but I know it is for my good.

How marvelous is Your name.

Although our sins testify against us, O LORD,

do something for the sake of Your name.

For our backsliding is great; we have sinned against You. Jeremiah 14:7

OUR GOD FOR EVER AND EVER

אֱלֹהֵינוּ עוֹלָם וָעֶד

Eh-lo-hay-noo O-lahm Vah-ehd

For this God is our God for ever and ever.

Psalm 48:14a

When I am afraid, I think upon You,

that You have been Our God For Ever and Ever,

Eh-lo-hay-noo O-lahm Vah-ehd.

There is much comfort in knowing

that You have been in all of my yesterdays, and

You will be in all of my tomorrows.

Just knowing this gives me peace that passes understanding.

Thank You for allowing me to know

Your wonderful name.

For the sake of Your name, do not despise us. Jeremiah 14:21a

OUR HOPE

Teek-vah-tay-noo

Paul, an apostle of HaMashiach Yeshua Messiah Jesus,
by the command of God our Savior and of HaMashiach
Yeshua Messiah Jesus, our hope.

1 Timothy 1:1

How I praise You, Father, for this marvelous hope
that we have in Jesus. What a blessing to know that
no matter how dark the storm, how treacherous the
waters, You will always bring me through. As Jesus
overcame death and the grave, You will give me the
power to overcome, too. How wonderful You are,
Our Hope, Teek-vah-tay-noo!

OUR JUDGE

Shof-tay-noo

For the LORD is our judge,

the LORD is our lawgiver,

the LORD is our king,

It is He who will save us.

Isaiah 33:22

How thankful I am that You are Our Judge,

Shof-tay-noo. Even though I am fearful of You,

it is a godly reverent fear of You; yet I do not

fear to approach You. For I am thankful that it

is not based on my righteousness that I am judged,

for I have no righteousness of my own.

All I have is because of Yeshua's righteousness.

I am in good standing with God all because of Yeshua.

How I praise Your name!

"It is Jesus Yeshua's name and the faith that comes through Him

that has given this complete healing to him,

as You can all see." Acts 3:16

OUR KING

מַלְכֵּנוּ

Mahl-kay-noo

For the LORD is our judge,

the LORD is our lawgiver,

the LORD is our king;

it is He who will save us.

Isaiah 33:22

You are Our King, Mahl-kay-noo, our Master
over everything in our lives. That is a good
place for us to be, submissive to Your will.
There is much freedom and liberality in this
open place; it is a safe place. When I abide
under Your sovereign power, I feel safe,
and I come to know Your peace, Your Shalom.
How I love Your name.

OUR LAWGIVER

M'kho-k'kay-noo

For the LORD is our judge,

the LORD is our Lawgiver.

Isaiah 33:22a

Thank You for giving us Yeshua, Our Lawgiver,
M'kho-k'kay-noo. He gave the Law and He completes
the Law. Thank You so much for showing, in Your
life, that Love is the fulfillment of the Law. I want
more of You in my life. I need more of You in my life.
How I praise Your wonderful name!

"The blessing of the LORD be upon you; we bless you
in the name of the LORD." Psalm 129:8

OUR LORD AND SAVIOR

אֲדֹנֵינוּ וּמוֹשִׁיעֵינוּ

Ah-do-nay-noo Oo-mo-shee-ay-noo

But grow in the grace and knowledge of our Lord and Savior
Yeshua HaMashiach Jesus Christ.
To Him be glory both now and forever! Amen.

2 Peter 3:18

All glory to Yeshua, Our LORD and Savior,
Ah-do-nay-noo Oo-mo-shee-ay-noo.
Thank You for the privilege of living this exchanged life.
You are LORD, You are my Savior; what I could not do,
You did for me at the cross.
Thank You for giving me forgiveness of my sins.
I owe my life to You.

OUR MASTER

Ah-do-nay-noo

The disciples went and woke Him, saying,
"Master, Master, we're going to drown!"
Luke 8:24a

If we are to be servants, then may our master be perfect, and
that You are, Our Master, Ah-do-nay-noo;
how excellent are Your mysterious ways.
It is our heart's desire to please You in all we do.
Thank You for Your wonderful eternal plan
for our lives. How excellent is Your name!

OUR ONLY SOVEREIGN AND LORD

אֲדֹנֵינוּ מֹשֵׁל יָחִיד

Ah-do-nay-noo Mo-shell Yah-kheed

For certain men whose condemnation was written about long ago

have secretly slipped in among you.

They are godless men, who change the grace of

our God into a license for immorality

and deny Jesus Christ our only Sovereign and Lord.

Jude 1:4

Even today, there are people in our midst who deny You. May I always

be mindful of these evil godless men and women.

Thank You for all the help You give against our enemies.

I called on Your name, O LORD,

from the depths of the pit. Lamentations 3:55

OUR PASSOVER

Pees-khay-noo

Purge out therefore the old leaven, that ye may be
a new lump, as ye are unleavened.
For even Messiah our Passover is sacrificed for us.
1 Corinthians 5:7 KJV

With the Blood of an unblemished lamb, the children of
Israel were spared the wrath of the Angel of Death.
And with the Blood of the unblemished Passover,
Pees-khay-noo, we, Your children, are spared the wrath
of eternal death. Because of Our Messiah, the Passover,
we live. How I praise Your name!

Let every creature praise His holy name for ever and ever.
Psalm 145:21b

OUR PEACE

שְׁלוֹמֵנוּ

Sh-lo-may-noo

For He Himself is our peace, who has made the
two one and has destroyed the barrier,
the dividing wall of hostility.
Ephesians 2:14

Thank You for the peace that You give; it is a peace
not from man, but from You. You end hostility between
Jew and Gentile, man and woman. We are Eh-chad, One,
in Yeshua. Thank You for being Our Peace, Sh-lo-may-noo.

The LORD God Almighty, the LORD is His name of renown! Hosea 12:5

OUR REDEEMER

Go-ah-lay-noo

Our Redeemer—the LORD Almighty is His name—

is the Holy One of Israel.

Isaiah 47:4

I get excited when I think of Your work at Calvary.

You won us the victory over death, hell and the grave.

What a Redeemer You are!

OUR REDEEMER FROM OF OLD

גֹּאֲלֵנוּ מֵעוֹלָם

Go-ah-lay-noo May-o-lahm

You, O LORD, are our Father,

our Redeemer from of old is Your name.

Isaiah 63:16B

Thank You for paying the ultimate price to redeem
us from the enemy of our souls. You paid the ultimate
price—Your life, so that we may live. You are
Our Redeemer from of Old, Go-ah-lay-noo May-o-lahm;
how thankful we are for Your wonderful plan and for
Your wonderful name.

It is good to praise the LORD and make music
to Your name, O Most High. Psalm 92:1

OUR ROCK

צוּרֵנוּ

Tsoo-ray-noo

For their rock is not like our Rock,

as even our enemies concede.

Deuteronomy 32:31

Even our enemies can see that there is something different about

You, Our Rock, Tsoo-ray-noo.

There is none like You.

You are strong, You are mighty,

You are Our Rock!

PHYSICIAN

Ro-fay

Is there no balm in Gilead? Is there no physician there?
Why then is there no healing for the wound of My people?
Jeremiah 8:22

You are all the Physician I need for my wounds.
You, Physician, Ro-fay, are my healer,
the healer of broken hearts, broken lives.
Thank You that You make me well.

PIERCED

מְחֹלָל

M'kho-lahl

But He was pierced for our transgressions,

He was crushed for our iniquities.

Isaiah 53:5a

It was prophesied that this would happen to You,

yet it is still painful to think upon.

You were Pierced, M'kho-lahl,

Pierced for me, for my sins:

for my lying, for my stealing.

Thank You.

PLANT OF RENOWN

מַטָּע לְשֵׁם

Mah-tah L'Shaym

And I will raise up for them a plant of renown,
and they shall be no more consumed with hunger
in the land, neither bear the shame
of the heathen anymore.

Ezekiel 34:29 KJV

You are the Plant of Renown,
Mah-tah L'Shaym, who supplies all that
I will ever need.
The Everlasting Plant, the Righteous Root,
forever giving life.
How I bless Your name.

PRIEST

כֹּהֵן

Kho-hayn

For it is declared:
"You are a priest forever,
in the order of Melchizedek."
Hebrews 7:17

What a blessing it is to know that I do not have to go through
another intermediary to have my prayers heard. Yeshua
Jesus is our advocate, our high Priest, and He is at the
Father's right hand interceding always.
What a glorious God!

He who forms the mountains, creates the wind, and reveals His thoughts to man,
He who turns dawn to darkness, and treads the high places of the earth—
the LORD God Almighty is His name. Amos 4:13

PRINCE OF PEACE

שַׂר-שָׁלוֹם

Sar Shalom

For to us a child is born, to us a son is given,

and the government will be on His shoulders.

And He will be called Wonderful Counselor, Mighty God,

Everlasting Father, Prince of Peace.

Isaiah 9:6

One day there will be peace on earth. You will usher it forth, dear Prince of Peace, Sar Shalom. Make me an agent of Your peace.

RABBONI

רַבּוּנִי

Rah-bo-nee

Jesus Yeshua said to her,

"Mary."

She turned toward Him and cried out in Aramaic,

"Rabboni!" (which means Teacher).

John 20:16

You are Teacher, Rabboni, Rah-bo-nee. Thank You
that You instruct us in the way that we should live.
You show us how to live in obedience according to
God's love, with everything bathed in love.
What a wonderful God You are!

RANSOM

Ko-fehr

"For even the Son of Man did not come to be served,
but to serve, and to give His life as a ransom for many."
Mark 10:45

You paid the penalty of my sin on the cross;
You are my Ransom, Ko-fehr.
Thank You for not only covering my sins, but
doing away with my sins
when You died upon that tree.
Thank You for this marvelous mystery!

REFINER'S FIRE

כְּאֵשׁ מְצָרֵף

K-aysh M-tsah-rayf

But who can endure the day of His coming?

Who can stand when He appears?

For He will be like a refiner's fire or a launderer's soap.

Malachi 3:2

Burn out all of the dross in me, Refiner's Fire, K-aysh M-tsah-rayf.

Apply Your fire to my very being, that all evil will be purged from me.

I want to be clean in thought, word and deed.

Thank You for the fire of Your Holy Spirit that enables me to walk

as You desire me to walk, all because of Yeshua,

our Refiner's Fire.

REFUGE AND STRENGTH

מַחֲסֶה וָעֹז

Mah-kha-seh Vah-oze

God is our refuge and strength,
an ever-present help in trouble.
Psalm 46:1

When I am afraid, I run to You. You are my Refuge,
the One to whom I run. I find shelter
under the shadow of Your wings.
With You there is safety.

"Do not swear falsely by My name and so
profane the name of Your God. I am the Lord."
Leviticus 19:12

REFUGE FOR THE NEEDY

מָעוֹז לָאֶבְיוֹן

Mah-oz Lah-ehv-yone

You have been a refuge for the poor, a refuge for the needy in His distress,

a shelter from the storm and a shade from the heat.

Isaiah 25:4a

I am needy, LORD. Thank You for making me needy

so that I can come to You and pray.

Not only do You hear my needy prayers,

You answer!

REFUGE FOR THE POOR

מָעוֹז לַדָּל

Mah-oze Lah-dahl

You have been a refuge for the poor,

a refuge for the needy in his distress,

a shelter from the storm and a shade from the heat.

Isaiah 25:4a

I am needy, LORD. Thank You for making me poor in spirit.

When I am poor in spirit, You fill me up.

I praise You, Mah-oze Lah-dahl, dear Refuge for the Poor.

When I am poor, You make me rich.

All the nations may walk in the name of their gods;

we will walk in the name of the LORD our God for ever and ever. Micah 4:5

REJECTED BY MEN

חֲדַל אִישִׁים

Khah-dahl Ee-sheem

He was despised and rejected by men,
a man of sorrows, and familiar with suffering.

Isaiah 53:3a

When I face rejection, I look to You,

Rejected by Men, Khah-dahl Ee-sheem.

I find comfort in You.

RESURRECTION AND THE LIFE

הַתְּקוּמָה וְהַחַיִּים

Haht-koo-mah V'hah-khy-eem

Jesus said to her, "I am the resurrection and the life.
He who believes in Me will live, even though he dies."
John 11:25

Thank You, LORD.

I do not have to understand everything about You to walk with You.

Thank You that I can come to You by faith.

I have eternal life because of You.

What hope You give me because You are

the Resurrection and the Life!

REVEALER OF MYSTERIES

גָּלֵה רָזִין

Gah-lay Rah-zeen

The king said to Daniel, "Surely your God
is the God of gods and the Lord of kings and
a revealer of mysteries."

Daniel 2:47a

It is not important to me to know all of the answers;
it is more important to know the One who has the
answers, and that is You, the Revealer of mysteries,
Gah-lay Rah-zeen. Life is a mystery, Yeshua is a
mystery, Your love is a mystery—yet I am at peace
when I rest in the knowledge that I know You, and
most importantly, You know me.

Save us, O LORD our God, and gather us from the nations,
that we may give thanks to Your holy name
and glory in Your praise.

Psalm 106:47

RIGHTEOUS BRANCH

צֶמַח צַדִּיק

Tseh-mahkh Tsah-deek

"The days are coming," declares the LORD,
"when I will raise up to David a righteous branch,
a King who will reign wisely and do what is
just and right in the land."
Jeremiah 23:5

It doesn't make sense to some that You are a
Righteous Branch, Tseh-mahkh Tsah-deek.
But Your word says that if I abide in You, I
shall know the truth, and the truth shall set me free.
How thankful I am to know You, the One who
gives me eternal life; but You also set me free by
helping me to follow the right way—the way of the
Righteous Branch. How I praise Your lovely name.

RIGHTEOUS FATHER

אָבִי הַצַּדִּיק

Ah-vee Hah-tzah-deek

"Righteous Father, though the world does not know You, I know You,

and they know that You have sent Me."

John 17:25

What a comfort it is to know that You, Father, are

Righteous. You are always right.

In this crazy upside-down world,

You make my world right-side up.

How I praise Your name!

He will stand and shepherd His flock in the strength

of the LORD, in the majesty of the name

of the LORD His God. And they will live securely,

for then His greatness will reach to the ends

of the earth. Micah 5:4

RIGHTEOUS JUDGE

Sho-fate Tzeh-dehk

Now there is in store for me the crown of righteousness, which the Lord,

the righteous Judge, will award to me on that day—and not only to me,

but also to all who have longed for His appearing.

2 Timothy 4:8

How I long for Your appearing, LORD!

You are the Righteous Judge. I can trust You

to vindicate me in the presence of my foes.

I long to see You.

RIGHTEOUS ONE

Hah-tzah-deek

My dear children, I write this to you so that you will not sin.

But if anybody does sin, we have One

who speaks to the Father in our defense—Jesus Christ,

the Righteous One.

1 John 2:1

Yeshua, Jesus, thank You that I see in the flesh the model of

Righteousness.

Thank You that You are my guide; help me to pattern my life

after You.

I want to be like You, LORD!

"Then will I purify the lips of the peoples,

that all of them may call on the name of the LORD

and serve Him shoulder to shoulder." Zephaniah 3:9

ROCK

צוּר

Tsoor

"For who is God besides the LORD?

And who is the Rock except our God?"

Psalm 18:31

There is nothing around me that supports like You, the Rock, Tsoor.

Everything else is shifting sand;

You are the only Rock upon which I need to stand.

There is no unsteadiness with You.

How I praise You, for You are all I need.

Thank You for the security that is found in You.

And I will do whatever you ask in My name, so that

the Son may bring glory to the Father. John 14:13

ROCK OF ISRAEL

צוּר יִשְׂרָאֵל

Tsoor Yis-rah-el

And you will sing as on the night you celebrate

a holy festival; your hearts will rejoice

as when people go up with flutes to the mountain of the LORD,

to the Rock of Israel.

Isaiah 30:29

My heart rejoices in You, O Rock of Israel.

You were a Rock to Israel;

You are my Rock.

How I praise Your name!

ROCK OF OUR SALVATION

צוּר יִשְׁעֵנוּ

Tsur Yeesh-ay-noo

Come, let us sing for joy to the LORD;

let us shout aloud to the Rock of our salvation.

Psalm 95:1

There is no rock like You, dear Rock of our Salvation,

Tsur Yeesh-ay-noo.

There is salvation in the name of Yeshua:

You are the Rock that we can run to, for

You save us.

You save us from our enemies, from our friends,

and yes, even from ourselves.

Thank You for saving me from eternal damnation.

How I praise Your name!

ROOT OF DAVID

שֹׁרֶשׁ דָּוִד

Sho-resh Dah-veed

Then one of the elders said to me,

"Do not weep! See, the Lion of the tribe of Judah,

the Root of David, has triumphed."

Revelation 5:5

What a divine mystery, that You are from the line of

David. Glorious lineage!

Human yet divine.

Then those who feared the LORD talked with each other,

and the LORD listened and heard.

A scroll of remembrance was written in His presence

concerning those who feared the LORD and honored His name. Malachi 3:16

ROSE OF SHARON

חֲבַצֶּלֶת הַשָּׁרוֹן

Kha-vah-tseh-let Hah-Shah-ron

"I am a rose of Sharon, a lily of the valleys."
Song of Solomon 2:1

How beautiful You are to me, dear LORD. Words cannot
express the beauty that is found in You. Just as a true
description of a rose cannot really be told, neither can a true
description of You really be told. How lovely You are,
Rose of Sharon, Kha-vah-tseh-let Hah-Shah-ron.

RULER OF GOD'S CREATION

רֵאשִׁית בְּרִיאַת הָאֱלֹהִים

Ray-sheet B'ree-aht Hah-Eh-lo-heem

"To the angel of the church in Laodicea write:

These are the words of the Amen, the faithful and true witness,

the ruler of God's creation."

Revelation 3:14

You were there at creation. You were there at the beginning.

In the beginning was the Word.

In the beginning there was You!

RULER OVER ISRAEL

מוֹשֵׁל בְּיִשְׂרָאֵל

Mo-shayl B'Yees-rah-el

"But you, Bethlehem Ephrathah,

though you are small among the clans of Judah,

out of you will come for me

one who will be ruler over Israel,

whose origins are from of old, from ancient times."

Micah 5:2

You will reign one day over Israel.

One day, all Israel will look upon You

and see You in Your glory.

May You have compassion upon Israel.

The crowds that went ahead of Him and those that followed shouted, "Hosanna
to the Son of David! Blessed is he who comes in the name of the Lord!" Matthew 21:9

SAVIOR

מוֹשִׁיעַ

Mo-shee-ah

"I, even I, am the LORD, and apart from Me there is no savior."
Isaiah 43:11

Savior…Redeemer…LORD.
You laid down Your perfect sinless life so that I might be saved.
Thank You!
You took my place on the cross.
You suffered, died, rose on the third day, and now
You sit at the Father's right hand.
Even though I shall never fully understand this,
I accept it by faith.
Mo-shee-ah, Savior, may I live this day as only
You would live it.
Help me to be a vessel of love to all that I meet.
Thank You, my Savior, my deliverer, my LORD.

SAVIOR OF ALL MEN

הַמּוֹשִׁיעַ לְכָלאָדָם

Hah-mo-shee-yah L'kohe Ah-dahm

We have put our hope in the living God,
who is the Savior of all men,
and especially of those who believe.
1 Timothy 4:10b

Hallelujah! You aren't the savior of just a few people.

You are the Savior of All Men! And Women!

Everyone.

How we praise Your name!

"Blessed is the king who comes in the name of the Lord!

Peace in heaven and glory in the highest!" Luke 19:38

SAVIOR OF THE BODY

הַמוֹשִׁיעַ לִגְוִיָּתוֹ

Hah-Mo-shee-yah Leeg-vee-yah-toe

For the husband is head of the wife,

as also Christ is head of the church:

and He is the savior of the body.

Ephesians 5:23 NKJV

By Your righteous deed, You became

Savior of the Body.

Help me to submit to You, as You submitted

Your will to the Father.

What a wonder You are!

SAVIOR OF THE WORLD

מוֹשִׁיעַ הָעוֹלָם

Mo-shee-yah Hah-O-lahm

They said to the woman,

"We no longer believe just because of what you said;

now we have heard for ourselves, and we know that this Man really is

the Savior of the world."

John 4:42

Lord, just as You knew all about that woman,

You know about me.

Knowing You is all I need.

You are my Savior; You are the Savior of the World.

Help us to live in joy for what You have done for us.

SCEPTER

Shay-veht

"A star will come out of Jacob; a scepter will rise out of Israel."

Numbers 24:17b

You are the Scepter that arose out of Israel.

You rose on the third day.

This is a great mystery:

Yeshua lived,

Yeshua died,

Yeshua rose,

Yeshua will come again.

Marvelous Scepter, marvelous Shay-veht.

SECOND MAN

Hah-ah-dahm Hah-shay-nee

The first man was of the dust of the earth,
the second man from heaven.
1 Corinthians 15:47

Even though I was born of the first man, Adam,
I am born again of the Second Man, Hah-ah-dahm
Hah-shay-nee; this Second Man is Yeshua, Jesus.
Forgive my "first-man" tendencies, for I desire
to have only "Second-Man" responses. I thank You
that my new nature is Spirit-led, all because of
You, LORD. How I love Your name!

Then will I ever sing praise to Your name
and fulfill my vows day after day. Psalm 61:8

SEED OF DAVID

זֶרַע דָּוִד

Zeh-rah Dah-veed

Remember that Yeshua HaMashiach,
of the seed of David,
was raised from the dead
according to my gospel.
2 Timothy 2:8 NKJV

Just as it was prophesied in the Holy Scriptures, You did come from
the Seed of David. What wonders are bestowed upon us who believe;
what a wonderful plan did God have from the beginning. You are a
wonder, O Seed of David, Zeh-rah Dah-veed. I praise Your name.

SHADE FROM THE HEAT

צֵל מֵחֹרֶב

Tzayl May-kho-rehv

You have been a refuge for the poor,
a refuge for the needy in his distress,
a shelter from the storm
and a shade from the heat.

Isaiah 25:4a

When tough times have come upon me, times that are
pressure-filled, You are my Shade from the Heat.
What a wonder You are!

So Saul stayed with them and moved about
freely in Jerusalem, speaking boldly
in the name of the Lord. Acts 9:28

SHELTER FROM THE STORM

מַחְסֶה מִזֶּרֶם

Makh-seh Mee-tzeh-rehm

You have been a refuge for the poor,

a refuge for the needy in his distress,

a shelter from the storm

and a shade from the heat.

Isaiah 25:4a

Storms come and storms go in my life. What a protection

You are, LORD. You are the Shelter from the Storm.

I praise Your wonderful name.

SHEPHERD

Ro-ee

The LORD is my shepherd,

I shall not be in want.

Psalm 23:1

You are my Shepherd, my companion,

Herdsman, Tender of the Flock, dear Ro-ee.

Without You, Your people would perish.

How I praise You, O Gentle Shepherd, for the blessed way

that You lead me and guide me.

You make me to lie down in green pastures.

Surely my cup overflows.

I will proclaim the name of the LORD.

Oh, praise the greatness of our God!

Deuteronomy 32:3

SHEPHERD OF ISRAEL

רֹעֵה יִשְׂרָאֵל

Ro-eh Yis-rah-el

Hear us, O Shepherd of Israel,

You who lead Joseph like a flock;

You who sit enthroned between the cherubim, shine forth.

Psalm 80:1

To think that the One whose presence dwelt

between the cherubim

comes to dwell with me—

this astounds me, LORD.

How blessed I am to be led by the

Shepherd of Israel, Ro-eh Yis-rah-el.

Praises always to Your name.

SHIELD

Mah-gayn

As for God, His way is perfect;

the word of the LORD is flawless.

He is a shield

for all who take refuge in Him.

Psalm 18:30

You are my defense, my Shield, when enemies come upon me.

I will look up to You and not be afraid, for You are with me

and You will protect me.

Always!

Then Paul answered, "Why are you weeping and breaking my heart? I am ready not

only to be bound, but also to die in Jerusalem for the name of the Lord Jesus."

Acts 21:13

SLOW TO ANGER

אֶרֶךְ אַפַּיִם

Eh-rehk Ah-py-eem

The LORD is compassionate and gracious,
slow to anger, abounding in love.
Psalm 103:8

There are many times that I do wrong of which I know;
there are many times that I do wrong of which I know not.
Thank You for being Slow to Anger.
I deserve Your wrath, yet You give me Your love,
all because of Yeshua!

SMITTEN BY GOD

מֻכֵּה אֱלֹהִים

Moo-kay Eh-lo-heem

Yet we considered Him stricken,

Smitten by God, and afflicted.

Isaiah 53:4b NKJV

Smitten by God, Moo-kay Eh-lo-heem.

Not a desirable picture painted for us,

yet You died for me.

I thank You for laying down Your life for me.

Help me to live for You.

SON

Ben

No one knows about that day or hour,
not even the angels in heaven, nor the Son, but only the Father.
Matthew 24:36

So many people try to guess when Yeshua will return,
but only the Father knows when the Son will return.
That is good enough for me; that gives me peace.

You were washed, you were sanctified,
you were justified in the name of the Lord Jesus
the Messiah and by the Spirit of our God. 1 Corinthians 6:11

SON OF DAVID

Ben Dah-veed

As Yeshua Jesus went on from there, two blind
men followed Him, calling out,
"Have mercy on us, Son of David!"
Matthew 9:27

Scripture foretells that You would be from the
root of David, and Your ancestry proves You are.
What a great plan was made by God for all mankind.
How I love You, Son of David, Ben Dah-veed.

"O Lord, listen! O Lord, forgive! O Lord, hear and act!
For Your sake, O my God, do not delay, because Your city
and Your people bear Your name!" Daniel 9:19

SON OF GOD

בֶּן אֱלֹהִים

Ben Eh-lo-heem

Then those who were in the boat worshiped Him, saying,

"Truly You are the Son of God."

Matthew 14:33

Mysterious wonder! How You, Yeshua, are the Son of God.

I accept this by faith. I believe; one day I shall see.

my eyes will behold You, the Son of God,

Ben Eh-lo-heem.

I cannot wait to be with You face to face!

SON OF JOSEPH

Ben Yo-sayf

Philip found Nathanael and told him,

"We have found the one Moses wrote about in the Law,

and about whom the prophets also wrote—

Jesus of Nazareth, the son of Joseph."

John 1:45

Son of God, yet Son of Joseph, Ben Yo-sayf.

You had to come in the flesh in order to show us how to be like

You.

Majestic plan of God.

How I praise Your name!

SON OF MAN

Ben Hah-Ah-dahm

Yeshua Jesus replied,
"Foxes have holes
and birds of the air have nests,
but the Son of Man has no place to lay His head."
Matthew 8:20

Fully God, fully man. How I thank You for the mystery
of knowing You. And knowing that You know what it is
to be human, to struggle, to work, to feel, to love.
I am thankful that, by faith, I can accept this wonderful
mystery: You are the Son of Man, Ben Hah-ah-dahm.

SON OF MARY

Ben Meer-yahm

"Is this not the carpenter, the Son of Mary,
and brother of James, Joses, Judas, and Simon?"

Mark 6:3a NKJV

Son of Mary, Ben Meer-yam, You are God, yet Son of the woman.
I thank God for His wonderful, glorious plan.
One Young Jewish woman named Miriam said "Yes" to You,
and the rest is His-story.

SON OF THE BLESSED ONE

Ben Hah-m'vo-rakh

Again, the high priest asked Him,
"Are You the Messiah, the Son of the Blessed One?"
Mark 14:61

What a privilege to know You, the Messiah, the
Son of the Blessed One, Ben Hah-m'vo-rakh.
How I praise the Father for giving us You, his Son.
You show us how to love the Father,
by Your words and by Your deeds. May I live my
life with the same obedience that You displayed
here on earth. How I praise Your name.

You, O LORD, are our Father, our redeemer from of old
is Your name. Isaiah 63:16b

SON OF THE LIVING GOD

בֶּן אֱלֹהִים חַיִּים

Ben Eh-lo-heem Khy-eem

Simon Peter answered, "You are the Messiah,
the Son of the Living God."
Matthew 16:16

What a wonderful relationship You have to the Father:
You are his Son. And I am blessed to have
this relationship, too, not because of me
but because of Thee. I love You, LORD,
Son of the Living God,
Ben Eh-lo-heem Khy-eem.

SPIRIT OF GOD

Roo-akh El

The Spirit of God has made me;
the breath of the Almighty gives me life.
Job 33:4

Thank You, Spirit of God, Roo-akh El, for
making me, shaping me and molding me into
the person that You want me to be.
Thank You that Your spirit is gentle, yet strong, to help me
choose Your way.
Not by might, nor by power,
but only by Your Spirit: this is how I want to live.
Thank You, Roo-akh El.

SPRING OF LIVING WATER

מְקוֹר מַיִם חַיִּים

M'kor My-yeem Khy-yeem

"My people have committed two sins:
They have forsaken Me, the spring of living water. . ."
Jeremiah 2:13

You are the Spring of Living Water, M-kor My-yeem Khy-yeem.

All life comes from You.

If Your water source is not flowing through me, I have no life.

My goodness is from You.

How I love You, dear Spring of Living Water.

STONE

Eh-vehn

Now to you who believe,

this stone is precious.

But to those who do not believe,

"The stone the builders rejected has become the capstone."

1 Peter 2:7

What wonder! The Stone that others tripped over,

You allowed me to realize,

is the most precious Stone ever, Eh-vehn.

Thank You that more than riches, gold, diamonds, wealth—

You are the most precious Stone anyone could ever desire!

STRICKEN

נָגוּעַ

Nah-goo-ah

Yet we esteemed Him stricken,

Smitten by God, and afflicted.

Isaiah 53:4b NKJV

You were Stricken, Nah-goo-ah.

You were wounded.

You died for me.

Amazing suffering.

Amazing glory.

You are amazing.

STRONG FORTRESS

צוּר-מָעוֹז

Tsoor Mah-oz

Turn Your ear to me,

come quickly to my rescue; be my rock of refuge

a strong fortress to save me.

Psalm 31:2

O LORD, what a Rock You are, Tsoor Mah-oz, Strong Fortress.

How I thank You for Your strength in my life.

Be my strong rock, my Rock of Ages.

You are defense of my life.

How I praise You for that.

Help me to live today with the calm assurance and peace

of knowing that You are my strong defense.

"Therefore I will teach them—

this time I will teach them My power and might.

Then they will know that My name is the LORD."

Jeremiah 16:21

STRONG TOWER

מִגְדַּל־עֹז

Meeg-dahl Oz

The name of the LORD is a strong tower;

the righteous run to it and are safe.

Proverbs 18:10

LORD, in times of distress, help me to run to You,

O Strong Tower, Meeg-dahl Oz.

You are my protection amid the storms of life.

Thank You for Your sovereign protection and Your faithfulness.

SUN AND SHIELD

שֶׁמֶשׁ וּמָגֵן

Sheh-mesh Oo'Mah-gayn

For the LORD God is a sun and shield; the LORD bestows favor and honor;

no good thing does He withhold from those whose walk is blameless.

Psalm 84:11

You protect me, yet You shine down upon me. Usually, one wants to be shielded from

the sun, yet You are my Sun and Shield, Sheh-mesh

Oo'Mah-gayn. Thank You that You give my life light. And thank You that You shield

me from forces that try to destroy me. Thank You that

You protect me from the darkness, and You give

me light. I love You, LORD.

"My name will be great among the nations, from the rising

to the setting of the sun. In every place incense

and pure offerings will be brought to My name, because

My name will be great among the nations,"

says the LORD Almighty. Malachi 1:11

SUN OF RIGHTEOUSNESS

שֶׁמֶשׁ צְדָקָה

Sheh-mesh Ts-dah-kah

But for you who revere My name,
the sun of righteousness will rise with healing in its wings.
And you will go out and leap like calves released from the stall.

Malachi 4:2

How thankful I am to be able to look at the

Sun of Righteousness, Sheh-mesh Ts-dah-kah.

You are more glorious than I could ever hope for.

Thank You for Your good plan for my life.

It is a plan for my future and my hope.

Thank You, LORD.

TABERNACLE OF GOD

מִשְׁכַּן אֱלֹהִים

Meesh-kahn Eh-lo-heem

And I heard a great voice out of heaven saying,

Behold, the tabernacle of God is with men, and He

will dwell with them, and they shall be His people,

and God Himself shall be with them, and be their God.

Revelation 21:3 KJV

When I think of You dwelling within me, it is almost too much

for me to understand. By faith, I accept all that there is about

You, for I know that You are with me, closer than my own

breath. You, Tabernacle of God, Meesh-kahn Eh-lo-heem,

are the source of constant wonder and joy to me.

How I praise Your name!

The nations will fear the name of the LORD. Psalm 102:15a

TEACHER

רַבִּי

Rah-bee

Then a teacher of the law came to Him and said,
"Teacher, I will follow You wherever You go."
Matthew 8:19

You are my Master, my Teacher, Rah-bee, and I want
to be Your best student. Please lead me in the way
that I should go, so that I may best learn Your precepts
and Your ways. Thank You for never letting me fail.
Thank You for continuing to guide me in the way Everlasting.

THE COMING ONE

Hah-bah

"Are You the Coming One, or do we look for another?"

Matthew 11:3 NKJV

What a glorious day it will be when You,

the Coming One, Hah-bah,

will return. Sometimes it is just so hard to wait,

yet we know that it will be worth it, when we see

You face to face. Until then, help us to be about

the Father's business, with joy in our hearts, with

full assurance that You indeed will come again.

How I praise Your name.

The cords of death entangled me, the anguish of the grave
came upon me; I was overcome by trouble and sorrow.
Then I called on the name of the LORD. Psalm 116:3-4a

THE FATHER

Hah-ahv

"I came from the Father and entered the world;
now I am leaving the world and going back to the Father."
John 16:28

What a wonderful Father You are! I can visit with You,
I can cry to You; You know me and You help me and
You love me.
You are a perfect Father!

THE GOD OF ABRAHAM, THE GOD OF ISAAC AND THE GOD OF JACOB

Eh-lo-hay Ahv-rah-ham, Eh-lo-hay Yeetz-khahk
Eh-lo-hay Yah-ah-cove

God also said to Moses,

"Say to the Israelites, 'The LORD, the God of your fathers—the

God of Abraham, the God of Isaac and the God of Jacob—has

sent me to you.' This is My name forever, the name by which

I am to be remembered from generation to generation."

Exodus 3:15

What an amazing God You are! You are the God of Abraham,

the God of Isaac and the God of Jacob, and

You are the God of me!

And whatever you do, whether in word or deed, do it all in the name of the Lord Jesus,

giving thanks to God the Father through Him. Colossians 3:17

THE GOD WHO ANSWERS BY FIRE

Hah-Eh-lo-heem Ah-share Yah-ah-neh Vah-aysh

"Then you call on the name of your god,

and I will call on the name of the Lord.

The God who answers by fire--He is God."

Then all the people said, "What you say is good."

1 Kings 18:24

There is none like You. There are times when You appear as a mystery and

You answer by fire. I cannot explain these times; these are holy moments.

But I thank You for Your answer by fire.

Nevertheless, God's solid foundation stands firm, sealed with this inscription: "The

Lord knows those who are His," and, "Everyone who confesses the name of the Lord

must turn away from wickedness." 2 Timothy 2:19

THE GOOD SHEPHERD

הָרֹעֶה הַטּוֹב

Hah-ro-eh Hah-tove

"I am the good shepherd."

John 10:14a

The Good Shepherd hears His sheep, He tends to His sheep,

He loves His sheep.

You are the wonderful Good Shepherd.

May I always be found in Your sheepfold.

THE GREAT GOD

הָאֵל הַגָּדֹל

Hah-ale Hah-gah-dol

For the LORD your God is God of gods and
Lord of lords, the great God, mighty and
awesome, who shows no partiality
and accepts no bribes.
Deuteronomy 10:17

I worship You because of who You are, not what
You do for me. I am thankful that there is no power
on earth greater than You, the Great God, Hah-ale
Hah-gah-dol. There is no love stronger than Yours,
there is no mercy more giving than Yours.
Thank You for Your love.

Brothers, as an example of patience in the face of suffering, take the prophets who
spoke in the name of the Lord. James 5:10

THE GREAT, MIGHTY AND AWESOME GOD

הָאֵל הַגָּדוֹל הַגִּבּוֹר וְהַנּוֹרָא

Hah-ayl Hah-gah-dole Hah-guee-bore v'Hah-no-rah

"Now therefore, O our God, the great, mighty and awesome God,
who keeps His covenant of love, do not let all this hardship seem
trifling in Your eyes--the hardship that has come upon us."
Nehemiah 9:32a

You are the Great, Mighty and Awesome God, and nothing catches
You by surprise. Thank You that You will come to my aid
when trouble surrounds me.

THE HEAD

Ha-Rosh

Instead, speaking the truth in love,
we will in all things grow up into Him who is the
Head, that is, Messiah.
Ephesians 4:15

Dear Father,

Thank You for this marvelous, mysterious plan in which
Yeshua, Jesus, is the Head, the Head of the body of believers.
Thank You for including me in this family.

I appeal to you, brothers, in the name of our Lord Jesus Christ, that all of you agree
with one another so that there may be no divisions among you and that you may be
perfectly united in mind and thought. 1 Corinthians 1:10

THE LAMB

Hah Seh

In a loud voice they sang: "Worthy is the Lamb, who was slain,
to receive power and wealth and wisdom
and strength and honor and glory and praise!"
Revelation 5:12

You are the Lamb of God, our Passover Lamb, our
Pesach Lamb, the Spotless, Sinless Lamb, the Lamb, Hah Seh.
Thank You for the example You left us of how to
lay our lives down, to surrender, and to open not our
mouths even when facing death. This is a mystery and
I cannot understand Your fathomless love, yet I accept it.
How I praise Your name!

For the sake of His great name the LORD will not
reject His people, because the LORD was pleased
to make you His own. 1 Samuel 12:22

THE LAST ADAM

הָאָדָם הָאַחֲרוֹן

Hah-ah-dahm Hah-ah-khah-ron

So it is written: "The first man Adam became
a living being"; the last Adam, a life-giving spirit.
1 Corinthians 15:45

In Adam, we all died, as he brought forth original sin.
In Yeshua, we all live, as He broke the curse of death
by the shedding of His blood, once and for all.
You, the Last Adam, Hah-ah-dahm Hah-ah-khah-ron,
give me life, and life eternal. How I love Your name!

THE LORD OF GLORY

אֲדוֹן הַכָּבוֹד

Ah-don Hah-Kah-vod

None of the rulers of this age understood it,
for if they had, they would not have crucified
the Lord of glory.

1 Corinthians 2:8

By faith, I accept this mystery of the exchanged life.
For You are the Lord of Glory, Ah-don Hah-Kah-Vod,
and You gave Your life for me. You are the
Innocent One who deserves glory. I am the guilty one
who deserves shame. Yet You took my place on the
cross so that I can live an abundant life now, as well
as live eternally. What a wonderful God You are.

"Everyone who calls on the name of the Lord will be saved." Romans 10:13

THE LORD IS MY STRENGTH AND MY SONG

עָזִּי וְזִמְרָת יָהּ

Ah-zee V'zeem-raht Yah

"The LORD is my strength and my song."

Exodus 15:2a

Just as the children of Israel sang to You, after
You delivered them from the hands of the Egyptians,
help me to remember to sing about Your deliverance
that You give to me, Ah-zee V'zeem-raht Yah,
The LORD is my Strength and my Song.
So many times You come through for me;
I am not worthy, but Oh how I praise You, LORD,
for You are worthy to receive all the glory, all the praise,
all the honor, all the power,
all the blessings–both now and forevermore.

"You shall not misuse the name of the LORD your God,
for the LORD will not hold anyone guiltless
who misuses His name."

Exodus 20:7

THE MESSIAH

Hah Mah-shee-akh

**The first thing Andrew did was to find his brother Simon
and tell him, "We have found the Messiah."
John 1:41**

Messiah, Hah Mah-shee-akh, the Anointed One.

You have come. You will come again.

I must confess that sometimes I just don't grasp the

fullness of Your character—who You really are.

But I am thankful that I do not need to fully understand You.

I just must believe by faith,

that You are everything God's word says You are,

and yet…

You are so much more.

THE ONE AND ONLY

Yah-kheed

The Word became flesh and made His dwelling among us.

We have seen His glory, the glory of the One and Only,

who came from the Father, full of grace and truth.

John 1:14

There is none like You;

You are the One and Only God.

Thank You that even though I do not understand You

and Your glory, I accept it by faith.

When this became known to the Jews and Greeks living in Ephesus, they were all
seized with fear, and the name of the Lord Jesus was held in high honor. Acts 19:17

THE ONLY WISE GOD

אֵל דֵּעוֹת

El Day-ote

To the only wise God be glory forever through Yeshua HaMashiach!

Amen.

Romans 16:27

Man may think he is smart, even smarter than You.

But You are the Only Wise God, El Day-ote.

One day, every knee shall bow and every tongue confess

that Yeshua HaMashiach is LORD!

THE RIGHTEOUS

Hah-tsah-deek

My little children, these things write I unto You,

that ye sin not. And if any man sin, we have an

advocate with the Father, Yeshua HaMashiach

Jesus the Messiah the righteous.

1 John 2:1 KJV

You are Righteous, You are Holy, You are Sinless,

You are God. No one can approach You without

the wonderful forever atonement of Yeshua Jesus

the Righteous, Hah-tsah-deek. How I thank You

for the Blood of Messiah Yeshua, Jesus the Messiah,

that His righteousness can be mine.

How I praise Your name.

And the LORD said, "I will cause all My goodness to pass

in front of You, and I will proclaim My name, the LORD,

in Your presence." Exodus 33:19a

THE TRUE VINE

גֶּפֶן אֱמֶת

Geh-fehn Eh-meht

"I am the true vine, and my Father is the gardener."
John 15:1

How wonderful it is to know that if I abide in You,
Yeshua, the True Vine, Geh-fehn Eh-meht,
You will bring forth fruit in my life. As long as I am
attached to You, I will grow. Thank You for this
most wonderful way to live. How I praise Your name.

THE TRUTH

Hah-eh-meht

Yeshua Jesus answered,

"I am the way and the truth and the life."

John 14:6a

Everyone these days seems to be searching for truth.
Yet You say You are the Truth, Hah-eh-meht,
and I have found Your words to be true. There is much
peace and assurance in knowing that You guide my life,
and Your ways are ways of peace for me, not destruction.
Not one good promise of Yours to the house of Israel
failed: they all came to pass (Joshua 21:45); and I
believe that not one promise to me will fail, if I walk
in Your ways. How wonderful is Your name!

If My people, who are called by My name, will humble themselves
and pray and seek My face and turn from their wicked ways, then
will I hear from heaven and will forgive their sin and will heal their
land. 2 Chronicles 7:14

THE WAY

Hah deh-rekh

Yeshua Jesus answered,
"I am the way and the truth and the life."
John 14:6a

Thank You, Father, for allowing me to know Yeshua Jesus,
the Way, Hah deh-rekh. When I stumble, when I fall,
thank You that You are there to show me the Way. I need
not worry about where I am going, when I am holding onto
Your hand: You know the Way, You are the Way.
How wonderful You are!

THE WORD

Hah-dah-vahr

In the beginning was the Word, and the Word

was with God, and the Word was God.

John 1:1

Dear Yeshua,

How I love Your Word. When I read Your Word,

I am reading You. You are the Word, Hah-dah-vahr.

Daily I need Your sustenance; daily I need Your Word to indwell me,

to lead me in the paths of righteousness.

So I welcome You into this place, my humble heart;

may You, the Word, Hah-dah-vahr,

enlighten my spirit and lead me in the way I should walk.

How wonderful You are!

Blessed is he who comes in the name of the LORD. Psalm 118:26a

THEIR TRUE PASTURE

נְוֵה-צֶדֶק

N'vay Tseh-dehk

"Whoever found them devoured them; their enemies
said, 'We are not guilty, for they sinned against
the LORD, their true pasture.' "
Jeremiah 50:7

As You were Israel's True Pasture, N'vay Tseh-dehk,
You are our pasture, our dwelling place.
When we come and dwell in Your presence,
there You feed us.
And how wonderful it is that You do not feed us weeds!
You give us the finest, and in abundance, too.
With You, my cup surely runs over with goodness.
I love Your name.

THIS JUST PERSON

הַצַּדִּיק הַזֶּה

Hah-tsah-deek Hah-zeh

When Pilate saw that he could not prevail at all, but rather that a tumult was rising, he

took water and washed his hands before the multitude, saying,

"I am innocent of the blood of this just Person."

Matthew 27:24 NKJV

Maybe Pilate was innocent, but I confess that I am guilty of Your death.

My sins put You on the tree.

You took my place.

I owe You my life; You are This Just Person,

Hah-tsah-deek Hah-zeh.

TRUE

אֱמֶת

Eh-meht

And they cried with a loud voice, saying,

"How long, O Lord, holy and true,

until You judge and avenge our blood on those who dwell on the earth?"

Revelation 6:10 NKJV

When so many people are searching yet finding what is false,

what a blessing to know You as True,

Eh-meht.

Whatever You say, I know that I can rely on Your word,

for You are True.

TRUE GOD

אֱלֹהִים אֱמֶת

Eh-lo-heem Eh-meht

But the LORD is the true God;

He is the living God, the eternal King.

Jeremiah 10:10a

Krishna, Buddha, Allah—false gods. They are dead.

They are in the grave.

You are alive.

You are the True God, Eh-lo-heem Eh-meht.

How wonderful is Your name!

TRUE LIGHT

Or Eh-meht

The true light that gives light to every man

was coming into the world.

John 1:9

Thank You, Father, for sending Yeshua,

the True Light, Or Eh-meht, into the world,

to light up this dark place.

Thank You, too, that He lights up the dark places in my life, and brings joy.

Thank You for Your mysterious wonderful ways.

They rejoice in Your name all day long; they exult

in Your righteousness. Psalm 89:16

UPRIGHT ONE

Yah-shahr

The path of the righteous is level;

O upright One, You make the way of the righteous smooth.

Isaiah 26:7

O Father, O Upright One, Yah-shahr,

You who dwell in righteousness, how I praise You.

Thank You that everything that You do is perfect and right.

There is no favoritism in You; just and true are all Your ways.

I thank You for Your blessings in my life.

WARRIOR

אִישׁ מִלְחָמָה

Eesh Meel-khah-mah

"The LORD is a warrior;
the LORD is His name."
Exodus 15:3

Thank You that it is You who fight all my battles.
You are the One who confronts my enemies.
How I praise You–You always gain the victory for me,
Eesh Meel-khah-mah, Warrior. How I love Your name!

WONDERFUL

Peh-leh

For to us a child is born, to us a son is given,

and the government will be on His shoulders.

And He will be called Wonderful...

Isaiah 9:6a

Wonderful, Peh-leh, a wonder.

You!

How thankful I am for the "extra-ordinariness" of You.

Your ways are higher than mine; how Wonderful

You are!

May I live today with the inner assurance that the

Wonderful God loves me.

In Judah God is known; His name is great in Israel. Psalm 76:1

WONDERFUL IN COUNSEL

הִפְלִא עֵצָה

Heef-Lee Ay-tsah

All this also comes from the LORD Almighty,

wonderful in counsel.

Isaiah 28:29

When I spend that time with You, what I come away with is the knowledge

that I need no one but You. I don't need a counselor, I don't need

a psychologist—all I need is You.

You are Wonderful in Counsel, Heef-lee Ay-tsah.

Sometimes I am astounded at the answers that You give me about my problems.

I know You gave them to me,

because I could never have come up with those same answers.

How I wish everyone could know You in this way!

How I praise Your name.

There he built an altar to the LORD and called on the

name of the LORD. Genesis 12:8b

WORD OF GOD

דְּבַר הָאֱלֹהִים

D'vahr Ha'Eh-lo-heem

He is dressed in a robe dipped in blood,
and His name is the Word of God.

Revelation 19:13

Just as You were in the beginning,

You are the Word of God, D'vahr Ha'Eh-lo-heem.

Help me to get to know You more, day by day,

reading and meditating on Your Word,

just sitting in Your presence.

How I love You, LORD.

WORD OF LIFE

דְּבַר הַחַיִּים

D'vahr Hah-Khy-yeem

That which was from the beginning, which we have heard,
which we have seen with our eyes, which we have looked at
and our hands have touched—this we proclaim concerning
the Word of Life.

1 John 1:1

You are life and You give life to all. How blessed I am to know
that I will know You forever, dear Word of Life, D'vahr
Hah-Khy-yeem. In You is life, and in You is the light of men.
Thank You that life is present in You and not death. I do not fear
to be in Your presence, for You make me feel more alive than
ever. I exalt Your wonderful name.

"Now I am about to build a temple for the Name of the LORD my God and to dedicate it to Him for
burning fragrant incense before Him, for setting out the consecrated bread regularly, and for making burnt offerings every morning and evening and on Sabbaths and New Moons and at the appointed feasts of the LORD our God. This is a lasting ordinance for Israel." 2 Chronicles 2:4

YAH

Yah

Sing to God, sing praises to His name;

Extol Him who rides on the clouds,

By His name Yah,

And rejoice before Him.

Psalm 68:4 NKJV

O YAH, may my praise be glorious to You!

I sing praises to Your name, YAH, for

You reign in the heavens, yet

You love me.

You love us!

Hallelujah!

Glory in His holy name;

let the hearts of those who seek the LORD rejoice. Psalm 105:3

You ARE THE GOD WHO SEES ME

אֵל רָאִי

El Ro-ee

She gave this name to the LORD who spoke to her:

"You are the God who sees me," for she said,

"I have now seen the One who sees me."

Genesis 16:13

To know that I know You, and that

You love me and see me, is wonderful.

You are the answer to all of my questions, El Ro-ee.

Thank You that I never have to search again.

You fill my cup to overflowing.

You are the One Who Sees me and loves me most.

I praise Your name.

YOUR EVERLASTING LIGHT

אוֹר עוֹלָם

Or O-lahm

The sun will no more be your light by day,

nor will the brightness of the moon shine on you,

for the LORD will be your everlasting light,

and your God will be your glory.

Isaiah 60:19

How I praise You, LORD, for Your light that penetrates my darkness.

Your Everlasting Light, Or O-lahm: You are

the Light of my life. And Your light in me shall be everlasting.

What a wonderful God You are. How I praise Your name!

Then I looked, and there before me was the Lamb,

standing on Mount Zion, and with Him

144,000 who had His name

and His Father's name written on their foreheads. Revelation 14:1

YOUR GLORY

תִּפְאַרְתֶּךָ

Teef-ahr-taych

The sun will no more be your light by day, nor will the brightness
of the moon shine on you, for the lord will be your everlasting
light, and your God will be your glory.

Isaiah 60:19

I have no good of my own; You are my glory. How I praise You,
Teef-ahr-taych, for Your Glory. How splendid is Your way,
how wonderful is Your name!

"The LORD has kept the promise He made." 2 Chronicles 6:10

YOUR HOLY SERVANT

עַבְדְּךָ הַקָּדוֹשׁ

Ahv-d'khah Hah-kah-doshe

Indeed Herod and Pontius Pilate met together
with the Gentiles and the people of Israel in this
city to conspire against your holy servant Jesus,
whom you anointed.

Acts 4:27

Yeshua, You gave us an example to follow.

You are God's Holy Servant.

Help me to be more like You.

"O Lord, let Your ear be attentive to the prayer of this
Your servant and to the prayer of
Your servants who delight in revering Your name." Nehemiah 1:11

YOUR HUSBAND

בַּעֲלַיִך

Vo-ah-ly-yeek

"For your maker is your husband—
the LORD Almighty is His name."
Isaiah 54:5a

LORD, how wonderful it is to have You as my Husband, Vo-ah-ly-yeek.
Yeshua, You are the closest One to me; I can be open and honest
with You, and You never ignore me, You never shun me,
You never turn away to read Your newspaper. Thank You for
Your unconditional love to me. How fulfilled I am.
You meet my every need—thank You for loving me so much.

And this is His command: to believe in the name of His Son,
Jesus Christ, Yeshua HaMashiach,
and to love one another
as He commanded us. 1 John 3:23

YOUR KING

Mahl-k'khem

"I am the LORD, your Holy One,
Israel's Creator, your King."
Isaiah 43:15

Everybody has a "king" in their life—it may be a job king,
a sports king, a shopping king, a vice king…yet everyone reports in.
How I thank You that You are my King.
my prayer is that when others look at my life, they would say
that Yeshua is Your King, Mahl-k'khem. You are the only
King whom I desire to serve.

YOUR NAME

Sheem-khah

All the earth bows down to You;

they sing praise to You,

they sing praise to Your name.

Psalm 66:4

Your Name is the Name above All Names.

How blessed I am to know Your Name.

How I praise Sheem-khah, Your Name.

There is healing in Your Name.

There is life in Your Name.

There is help in Your Name.

There is provision in Your Name.

There is power in Your Name.

Everything I need is in Your Name.

Praise the LORD.

Praise, O servants of the LORD,

praise the name of the LORD. Psalm 113:1

YOUR SAVIOR

מוֹשִׁיעֶךָ

Mo-shee-eh-khah

For I am the LORD, your God,

the Holy One of Israel, your Savior.

Isaiah 43:3a

How boundless is Your love towards me!

You knew I needed a Savior, so You brought me Jesus,

Yeshua.

I love You, Jesus.

"Naked I came from my mother's womb, and naked I will depart.

The LORD gave and the LORD has taken away;

may the name of the LORD be praised." Job 1:21

YOUR SHIELD AND HELPER

Mah-gayn Ehz-reh-kha

Blessed are you, O Israel! Who is like you, a
people saved by the LORD? He is your shield
and helper, and your glorious sword.

Deuteronomy 33:29a

I am continuously astounded by You, LORD. Even
when I know I have strayed, and I think that I deserve
Your wrath, You give me Your love. I shall not ask
why. It just makes me have more a heart of praise at
the wonder of Your love. Your Shield and Helper,
Mah-gayn Ehz-reh-kha, a fitting name of Yours
for Israel and for all people who love You.

But these are written that you may believe that Jesus Yeshua
is the Messiah the Christ, the Son of God, and that by believing,
you may have life in His name. John 20:31

BIBLIOGRAPHY

Complete Hebrew/English Bible, Hard Cover Original Hebrew; Old Testament, Hebrew Translation; New Testament, New King James Version English.

Nashville: Thomas Nelson Publishers, 1996.

The Holy Bible, New King James Version

Nashville: Thomas Nelson Publishers, 1985.

The Holy Scriptures

Jerusalem: Koren Publishers, 1997.

The New Testament in Hebrew and English

Edgware, Middlesex. England: The Society for Distributing Hebrew Scriptures, 1993.

The Quest Study Bible, New International Version

Grand Rapids: Zondervan Publishing House, 1994.

THE HOLY BIBLE, NEW INTERNATIONAL VERSION®, NIV®

Copyright © 1973, 1978, 1984 by International Bible Society®

Used by permission. All rights reserved worldwide.

A Hebrew-English Bible According to the Masoretic Text and the Jewish Publication Society 1917 Edition

© 2005 All Rights Reserved to Mechon Mamre for this HTML Version

http://www.mechon-mamre.org/p/pt/pto.htm

30541632R00207

Made in the USA
San Bernardino, CA
16 February 2016